*A Pair of Lawn Sleeves*

Thomas Firth Jones

# A Pair of
# Lawn Sleeves

A biography of William Smith

(1727-1803)

Chilton Book Company

Philadelphia · New York · London

❀ ❀ ❀

*"A gentleman who returned into town with Mr. Paine and me in our coach undertook to caution us against two gentlemen particularly; one was Dr. Smith, the provost of the College, who is looking up to government for an American episcopate, and a pair of lawn sleeves."*

John Adams
*Diary,* August 29, 1774

# ✿ Acknowledgments

My thanks to Carol Snyderman, William Smith's greatest fan and my greatest support with every phase of this book. To the librarians of the University of Pennsylvania, where most of this book was researched. To Edwin Wolf II of the Library Company, Murphy D. Smith, Jr., of the American Philosophical Society, Robert Bailey of Washington College, H. George Hamilton of the Franklin Institute, Ruth V. Stewart of the Huntingdon County Historical Society, and Dr. Edgar Richardson.

Annotated copies of this book will be given to the Library Company of Philadelphia, the Washington College Library, and the Library of Congress.

*for my mother, Louisa Wallis Jones*

# ✿ Contents

*A Pair of Lawn Sleeves*

# 1 ✿ Education

Few men are so fortunate as to discover an institution exactly suiting their tastes and ambitions, and most who do so are many years in the search. St. Augustine was not baptized until he was thirty-three, and Lincoln was near fifty before he recognized the indivisibility of the Union. Stalin had to conquer an institution and—with great patience and determination—make it his own; and both Henry Ford and the Great Buddha had to create from the void their own institutions. But William Smith had the great good fortune to be born into the Church of England.

The Church of England: sinister child of religious doubts and a king's lust, it was compromised from the start. With such a heritage, it wisely did not truck with theology, but concentrated on tinsel of the better and more enduring sort. It hid itself in elaborate but vague rituals, equally disconcerting to the papist and the dissenter, and defended itself with humor and condescension. Yet it held a core of believers and of unarticulated belief, and it bred its own saints: Cranmer thrusting his hand into the fire, and syphilitic Florence Nightingale.

Into this church where all was understood and nothing was said, William Smith fitted as few men have ever fitted an institution; and if he was not a saint, he was nonetheless a man of thought and feeling, a teacher of things most difficult to teach, an exemplar.

"Soft, polite, insinuating," said John Adams. "Adulating, sensible, learned, industrious, indefatigable; he has art enough, and refinement upon art, to make impressions. . . ." Adams, the provincial politician, was looking for holes in the vestments of Smith, an established luminary of the capital. He found them soon enough, and so did others: in fact, some said there were more holes than whole cloth. Smith could have been a great man, had he chosen to live by others' standards, rather than his own.

William Smith was born April 27, 1727, in Aberdeenshire, Scotland. His father, Thomas Smith, was a gentleman more by birth than by circumstance; and his mother, Elizabeth Duncan, did not live long enough to enjoy the success of her brother, Admiral Duncan, who destroyed the Dutch fleet at Camperdown and was made a viscount. Thomas Smith was a small landholder, who might well have worked his land himself, did not his gentility forbid it; and as early as 1735 the education of William, the elder son by his first marriage, was taken over by the Society for the Education of Parochial Schoolmasters.

William Smith entered King's College, Aberdeen, in 1743. The university was in Presbyterian hands, and most of his fellow Anglicans who attended aimed for holy orders, which was none too high a calling in that day. A young preacher could expect to spend some years in the house of a nobleman, saying grace before dinner but retiring before dessert, currying the horses, etc. Eventually, he might be given a parish and a meager benefice; but Smith, as a charity student, could hardly even aspire to that. Though he stayed at Aberdeen four years, and though he did what was required of a "bursar," he emerged without orders, and even without a degree. He went to Abernethy, near Perth, to become a parochial schoolmaster, as the Society twelve years earlier had forseen that he would.

His failure to take a degree may have been partly financial. His mother was now dead, and his father was married to a second wife who bore him at least three more children, to add to the three he had had by his first wife. Smith's sister Isabella, who never married, helped raise this second family, which absorbed all of Thomas Smith's little income. Of the six or more children, William was the only one who went to college at all, let alone graduated; and the poverty of these early years easily accounts for Smith's lifelong preoccupation with money: "Avaricious and covetous," Ezra Stiles, President of Yale, wrote of him. Benjamin Rush, his doctor in his last illness, was even more pointed: "He seldom paid a debt without being sued or without a quarrel. He was extremely avaricious and lived, after acquiring an estate of £50,000, in penury and filth."

The parish schools in Scotland were Presbyterian. Smith taught for three years in a parochial (Anglican) school, where wages and working conditions were even worse than they were in the parish schools. He then appeared in *Scots Magazine* as the author of a letter: he was, he said, president of a committee of Scottish schoolmasters applying to Parliament for a wage subsidy. A couple of months later Smith set out for London to plead the case, bearing a letter of introduction to the Archbishop of Canterbury.

Scotland had then enjoyed the same king as England for a hundred and fifty years, and the same parliament for a little over forty years. However, Scotland still had its own laws, and the Presbyterian Church was the established church there. Scottish Presbyterians tended to be loyal—though not enthusiastically so—to the Hanovers who, though boors, were at least Protestant boors; but Scottish Anglicans were likely to be loyal to the elegant, exiled Stuarts. Only four years earlier, while Smith was a student at Kings College, Prince Charles Edward had seen the end of his pretensions at Culloden, and Aberdeen itself had been in Jacobite hands for five months in the winter of 1745–46. To subsidize the wages of Anglican schoolmasters in Scotland would have been a step toward establishing the Church of England there, to the enragement of the loyal Presbyterians.

Archbishop Thomas Herring was a persuasive preacher and an able administrator, but he was not a religious fanatic. He listened to Smith politely, and he may even have offered him advice; but he did not recommend Smith's cause to Parliament, and no one else did either. Eventually Smith saw that his scheme must fail and, instead of returning to his teaching in Scotland, he took ship for America in March, 1751, as tutor to the two sons of Colonel Josiah Martin of Long Island.

It was an odd turnabout. Smith had been absorbed in Scottish education, and his letter to *Scots Magazine* had given a six-point scheme for the improvement of schoolmasters' livings, as well as something of his own educational philosophy. It is unlikely that he had ever been out of Scotland until he came to London, three months before. He had family and (assumedly) friends at home, and he had them nowhere else. Socially, a tutor stood no higher than a schoolmaster: both lived in other people's houses, not quite servants but definitely not gentry. But a New World tutor had many advantages, including eventual social mobility and immediate money: in Scotland, Smith had earned no more than £10 a year.

In addition to his young charges and his linens, he brought with him from England several letters of introduction, including one from Herring to the Lieutenant Governor of New York, and he soon established himself there as a minor literary figure and controversialist. Almost at once he began to publish poetry, at first in periodicals but later in pamphlet and even book form. "The Mock-Bird and the Red-Bird; an American Fable," "Epitaph, on Miss Philipse," and "Some Thoughts on Education" were among his verse efforts. *Indian Songs of Peace,* a book of poems with a long prose preface, was published in the spring of 1753. It is not to be supposed that, after two years' residence in the country, Smith had made himself master of an Indian language, let alone an Indian perspective; rather, the aboriginal posture was a masquerade, as an English poet might masquerade as a shepherd to write pastorals, without having his readers think him in any way intimate with sheep. The subjects of these early poems do show how quickly Smith identified himself with America.

Many of these poems, and most of what he wrote before he got his honorary D.D.'s in 1759, are signed "William Smith, M.A., Aberdeen." Why not? Hadn't he done the work for it, after all? And besides, who would ever check with a university that was three thousand miles away?

Where Smith got the money to publish these books and pamphlets is conjectural. Martin probably paid him about three times what he had earned in Scotland, but he no doubt also had some patronage from his New York literary friends, especially from the wife of the Lieutenant Governor, who was herself a dabbler in the arts. Possibly with help from those same friends, he published in April, 1753, an eighty-six page pamphlet, the most important literary work of his life, *A General Idea of the College of Mirania.*

After a prologue in heroic couplets, "supposed to have been spoken at the opening of the College of Mirania," Smith says that he has fallen in with Evander, a native of that Utopian province, and that Evander has given him an account of the college, which was founded for "forming a succession of sober, virtuous, industrious citizens, and checking the course of growing luxury," because "it is education alone which can mend and rectify the heart. . . .

"The object they always kept in sight, was the easiest, simplest, and most natural method of forming youth to the knowledge and exercise of private and public virtue; and therefore they did not scruple to reject some things commonly taught at colleges ["logic being in some disrepute among them"] to add others, and shorten or invert the order of others, as best suited their circumstances. They often had this sentence in their mouth, which I think, in other words, I have read in Tillotson, that the knowledge of what tends neither directly nor indirectly to make better men, and better citizens, is but a knowledge of trifles. It is not learning, but a specious and ingenious sort of idleness."

In Mirania, students entered college at fourteen, and five years later emerged with a knowledge of (of course) Latin and Greek, but also of merchants' accounts, algebra, geometry, astronomy, navigation, surveying, rhetoric, philosophy, poetry, oratory, and—in the fifth year—natural science and history, especially modern history. Fencing, dancing, and modern languages were also available to those who could pay extra for them. Morality and religion were taught when "proper opportunities" arose in the course of other studies; history, for instance, says Smith, "is nothing more than religion and philosophy taught by examples." Each year, all of the regular courses were taught by one professor, and each subject broached was taught in its entirety before another subject was broached, because keeping the subjects in their "natural order . . . renders the whole plan simple and regular." There followed a considerable discussion of why philosophy naturally preceded oratory, etc.

Evander included some description of teaching methods, which gave Smith an opportunity to describe how *he* taught, or would like to. In correcting compositions, "the professor is sensible that great judgment and art are required. Always remembering that they are youth, he is greatly careful not to discourage them by too much severity." Evander, speaking of his own college years, says that in the last year the professor "treated us more as his bosom friends and companions, than as his pupils and scholars; and often, when the season permitted, would lead us to the adjoining fields, to make the proper remarks on the different plants, trees. . . ." *A General Idea* was full of enthusiasm for teaching, and it was not feigned: all his life, teaching and real estate speculation were what most excited Smith's enthusiasm.

In the second half of *A General Idea*, Smith made

some suggestions about the site, buildings, and fund raising of a King's College then being projected for New York; and he sent a copy of it to Dr. Samuel Johnson of Connecticut, soon to become president of the embryonic Columbia, and to various New Yorkers interested in the founding of that college; but as they were clearly looking to Johnson to head Columbia, and as Smith was equally clearly looking for a job, the most important copy he sent out was the one addressed to Benjamin Franklin. Franklin, though not yet embarked on his national and international career, was then at the zenith of his Philadelphia career: forty-seven years old, retired from the business that now supported him, and devoting himself to innumerable philanthropies and didacticisms, among them the Academy of Philadelphia, which he hoped to raise to collegiate status. Several years before, Franklin had written *Proposals Relating to the Education of Youth in Philadelphia,* and Smith had borrowed from it generously for his *General Idea.* For Philadelphia, Franklin wanted an entirely practical institution, an "English school"; but to gain the support of as many subscribers as possible, he had proposed that students learn both "those things that are likely to be most useful and most ornamental, regard being had to the several professions for which they are intended."

Franklin, who felt that his ideas for a practical education had been watered in the Academy of Philadelphia by the adherents of classical education, was enthusiastic about *A General Idea.* He was equally enthusiastic about Smith, who covered the pamphlet with a letter saying that he tossed these proposals off without hope of personal gain, as he would soon be returning to England, where he expected to take holy orders and settle permanently. Smith did intend to return to take orders, but he certainly had no intention of settling in the £10 per annum motherland. However, he may already have been operating on the maxim which he later dared to state aloud: "To gain men, it is necessary not to respect them."

As soon as Franklin received the pamphlet, he wrote back, "If it suits you to visit Philadelphia, before your return to Europe, I shall be extremely glad to see and converse with you here. . . ." And after he had read it, he was even more accommodating: "I know not when I have read a piece that has so affected me. . . . You may depend on my doing all in my power to make your visit to Philadelphia agreeable to you." In these effusions he was joined by Richard Peters, provincial secretary to the absent Penn family, who wanted ten copies of the pamphlet for his own perusal, and William Allen, the rich chief justice of the province, who —being less of a reader—thought he could do with six.

Smith did agree to come. For one thing, he wanted to place the two Martin boys in the Academy before his departure for England; and for another, he was not used to receiving such invitations: barely two years before, he had been no more than a schoolmasters' lobbyist, hanging around Westminster in the hope of a five pound raise.

The twenty-six-year-old William Smith who came to Philadelphia—really for a job interview, though no one admitted it—was tall, but not otherwise distinguished looking. His hair was dark, his nose long and straight, his chin round and firm. He spoke and wrote with eloquence, and his conversation—he always retained a Scottish burr—was learned, witty, and persuasive. He had taste, and some real knowledge of music and art, as well as of literature, education, religion, and politics. If he was apt to be awkward, and if his dress and toilet were not as fastidious as they might have been, he more than made up for that with his conviction and with his enormous energy. Everyone was impressed with the young M.A. from Aberdeen.

The Philadelphia to which he came in late May, 1753, must have impressed Smith too. Already, it was incomparably the most important city in North America, and the next twenty years were to be its golden age, celebrated in its own time by every civilized nation, and looked upon since its time as a kind of Periclean Athens in the wilderness. On the eve of the Revolution, its population would be greater than any English-speaking city except London, and its shipping tonnage would be greater than Boston or Charleston, and far greater than New York. Its art and science and medicine and education would be admired throughout the world; and in 1753 the city—only seventy years old but already on the verge of its great era—was tremulous with anticipated glory, as if Franklin, in drawing electricity down from the clouds, had charged its very bricks and stones.

It is odd that so mediocre a site should have raised such a city in so short a time. The low, swampy junction of the Delaware and Schuylkill rivers was good land only when compared to the other sites William Penn might have chosen on the grant he had wheedled from Charles II in settlement of a debt to his father. The Schuylkill was navigable for only five miles and the Delaware for thirty miles above the city; and as commerce traveled on water, it was impossible that Philadelphia should develop an extensive, dependent hinterland. The Delaware below the city offered a tortuous ninety-six-mile channel, full of bars and islands, which was often frozen over several months of the year. The difficulty of navigation, both inland and marine, would have doomed Philadelphia in the nineteenth century, even if the Revolution and yellow fever had not; but in the eighteenth, when commerce was not the only consideration, the city flourished.

Simply, Philadelphia was free, when most cities— in America and everywhere in the world—were not. The idea of freedom, of toleration, was not original to William Penn ("His writings and his life," says Macaulay, "furnish abundant proof that he was not a man of strong sense."); but it was a surprisingly difficult idea for men of his era to grasp. Penn clung to it, even when opposed by his fellow Quakers, who often thought they could do with some theocracy in the Massachusetts manner. Thomas Penn, though sharper than his father, was not so sharp as to discount the idea of freedom; and therefore Pennsylvania prospered under his proprietorship, filling rapidly with Germans of many sects, with every kind of Englishman, with Scots, Irish, Scotch-Irish, Negroes, French, Spaniards, Swedes. Except for Rhode Island—and, perhaps, the Ottoman Empire— nowhere else in the eighteenth century was so much freedom to be had, and men craved it. It is no coincidence that Benjamin Franklin came from Boston to Philadelphia in 1723, and no coincidence that he stayed.

Smith's arrival, thirty years later, was a much better staged event than was Franklin's: he did not get lost behind Petty's Island, and he bore no loaves of bread. The Academy, which was then several years old, assembled to honor him, and some of his own verses were recited to him. He answered by writing the trustees "A

Poem on Visiting the Academy of Philadelphia, June, 1753." But more important, during his stay he seems to have made a dicker with Franklin.

Franklin hoped to raise the Academy to a college, for which the Academy would become a feeder. He needed the approval of the Penn family, which was not friendly to him, and more money than could be raised in Philadelphia. If Smith could raise the money in England (and particularly from the Penns who, after some lean years, were now making a bundle on their province), why then Smith could count on a teaching job at the Academy immediately, and the provostship of the college as soon as the charter was secured. It was quite a thought for a young man who, at that moment, held no college degree, that he should look forward to being provost of a college in the near future. The salary may or may not have been discussed: when it was settled, two years later, it turned out to be £200.

"Unfriended Merit," as Smith called himself in a letter to Franklin and Richard Peters, arrived in London in the middle of September, 1753. Whatever his merit, his unfriendedness was eased by letters from Peters, Franklin, William Allen, and the New York lieutenant governor, which in turn secured him the support of Archbishop Herring and Peter Collinson, best known to Americans for his electrical correspondence with Franklin. Collinson was primarily a botanist, concerned both with agriculture in England and the colonies and with the discovery and classification of new plants. The generous prices he paid for John Bartram's botanical drawings made possible Bartram's expeditions to Georgia and Florida. Collinson was a fellow of the Royal Society. "Mr. Smith is a very ingenious man," he wrote. "It is a pity but he was more solid and less flighty."

Smith had many tasks and errands in London. He
saw to the printing of an English edition of the *Ele-
menta Philosophica* by Columbia's Samuel Johnson,
embellishing it with a preface and a prayer of his own.
He also had printed his own *Indian Songs,* now enlarged and particularized as *The Speech of a Creek Indian.* Three months after his arrival, he had himself ordained a preacher of the Church of England. And
because, during his ten day stay in Philadelphia, Franklin had drawn him into a number of his schemes, he
now delivered an address to the Society for the Propagation of the Gospel on what he and Franklin considered the greatest of all dangers to Pennsylvania: German immigrants, or "Palatine boors," as Franklin
called them. The Society was already sending preachers
among the Pennsylvania Germans, and a hot time they
must have had of it, preaching to a people for whom
theological controversy was the only recognized recrea-
tion. Smith and Franklin now wanted the Society to
send teachers as well.

"The distressing prospect of approaching darkness
and idolatry" was among them, Smith warned. They
needed instruction "to form the social temper, to keep
up a sense of religion, and guide such a people in their
duty," because "liberty is the most dangerous of all
weapons, in the hands of those who know not the use
and value of it. . . . But further, education, besides
being necessary to support the spirit of liberty and commerce, is the only means for incorporating the foreign-
ers with ourselves, in the rising generation. The old can
be exhorted and warned. The young may be instructed
and formed." Specifically, they needed to be instructed
to be less "pacific" toward the Indians, perhaps even toward a certain "Creek" Indian. The Quakers were rec-
ognizedly bad soldiers, and someone had to push back

the Indians if the province was to continue to expand.
Eighteenth-century Pennsylvania Germans were
roughly of two kinds: the Lutherans and Dutch Re-
formed, who were rapidly integrating with the English
culture, and the sectarians—Dunkards, Moravians,
Mennonites, Schwenkenfelders, etc.—who, two hundred and fifty years later, are still resisting English
schools and English culture. Pastorius, their earliest
leader, had bought for them "a separate little province"
with Germantown as its capital, and they had been
there as long as the English had been in Philadelphia.
At first, under their charter from William Penn, they
had made their own laws and held their own courts;
and they continued to conduct their own schools. By
1754, they already had a distinctive history and a culture that reflected it, and they had a remarkable spokes-
man in Christopher Sauer the eldest, farmer, clockmaker, and publisher.

"Peters, Allen, Schmitt [sic], Franklin, and
Muhlenberg," said Sauer, were among those who "care
very little about religion, nor do they care about the
cultivation of mind of the Germans . . . but they are
mortified that they cannot compel others to protect
their goods." In his newspaper, *The High Dutch Pennsylvania Historiographer, or Collection of Important
News from the Kingdom of Nature and the Church,*
and in almanacs and pamphlets as well, Sauer and his
son and grandson blasted every scheme that "Schmitt
and Franklin" and their friends put forward for angli-
cizing the Germans.

However, Smith's main object in London was to
get approval of and support for the new college from
Thomas—son of William—Penn. Pennsylvania, from
its founding till the Revolution, was ruled not by the

king nor by such representative institutions as it had, but by William Penn and his descendants, who held it as a fief of the crown. Landholders were supposed to pay annual quitrents to the Penn family, and had only as much voice in government as the Penns granted them. Though we are taught that America was a democracy from the start (New England with its Mayflower Compact and town meetings, Virginia with its House of Burgesses), and that the king's attempt to rescind our democratic prerogatives caused the Revolution, the truth is that the American colonies, when they were governed at all, were governed by a hodgepodge of laws, edicts, and agreements, most of them more medieval than not, and differing from one colony to another. Pennsylvania in its first ninety years was a feudal state, and its representative institutions (General Assembly, Philadelphia City Council) were at the sufferance of its Lords Proprietary.

But feudal government requires a strong ruler, and Pennsylvania never had one. William Penn, even in his best days, was vain, bumbling, and capricious. He lived here only forty-five months out of the thirty-seven years between his acquisition of the province in 1681 and his death in 1718. In his last years, strokes and senility did not keep him from preaching to the Quakers and begetting more children, but they made him a worse proprietor than ever; and after he died the title to Pennsylvania was long contested among the children of his two marriages, his creditors, the Board of Trade, and an ex-steward to whom—in a more than usually obfuscated moment—Penn had signed over the whole province.

Meanwhile, Pennsylvania was ruled by an erratic succession of governors who fought with everybody. Probably the province would have fallen apart, had it not been for James Logan, a young secretary whom William Penn brought over on his second and final visit in 1698. When Penn returned to England, Logan stayed as provincial secretary, meaning land agent for the Penns. He lived until 1750 and was for many years the most astute and influential citizen of the province; but he never became governor because he was a nominal Quaker—and had to remain one, for fear of alienating the other Quakers—and as such he could not take the Test Act oath which was necessary to the assumption of royal office. All oaths were forbidden Quakers, and especially ones which swore to defend the king's domains. The same scruple long prevented Penn's sons from becoming governors and providing the leadership Pennsylvania needed.

Thomas Penn, the second son of William Penn's second marriage, was born in England in 1702. His childhood was clouded by his father's financial troubles, and at thirteen he was apprenticed to a mercer. However, in 1727 he and his brothers John and Richard triumphed in their litigation as heirs to their father and mother, now both dead, and assumed the ownership of Pennsylvania, which Logan was beginning to make profitable. John, the eldest, got half, and Thomas and Richard got a quarter each, and both John and Thomas visited Pennsylvania, where Thomas is said to have asked Conrad Weiser, the greying Indian agent and devout German sectarian, "Whether he was really accomplishing anything in this beastly wilderness, where there were neither good wines nor likely wenches."

John stayed only a few months, but Thomas must have found the wine and wenches because he stayed nine years. He was a good administrator ("How dost

do?" he would say to callers. "Please, the other door."),
but he was never able to reconcile the quarreling Pennsylvanians to himself or to each other. He left for England in 1741, intending to return, but he never did.
When John died in 1746, Thomas became three-quarter owner of the province and—true to his paternal heritage—he set himself up in style. At forty-nine, having long since discarded "the little distinction of dress" (i.e., plain clothes), he married the twenty-two-year-old Lady Juliana Femor, retired to the country, became a communicant of the Church of England, and spent the rest of his life begetting children.

Benjamin Franklin did not break with the Penns until 1755, but by 1753 he was already a considerable thorn in Thomas Penn's fattening side. Penn tried to buy him off by giving the Library Company an electrical apparatus for him to play with; but Franklin, the republican, was not so easily reconciled to his feudal lord. Yet his hopes for a college in Philadelphia depended on the money and the approval that only Penn could provide. Had Franklin himself come to England to solicit them, he would almost certainly have failed.

William Smith, on the other hand, was from his earliest days a lover of established institutions and those who ruled them. Two years afterward, when he was back in Philadelphia, he was to give Penn a sample of his sentiments: "What I can do shall always be at your service, while I am convinced of your attachment to the welfare of the province, and the preservation of the just rights of government, against a leveling and licentious race of republicans." Far from despising proprietary government, in later life he established a proprietorship of his own in Huntingdon, Pennsylvania, collected his quitrents, and made a pack of money on it.

After his first visit, Penn was so satisfied with him that he wrote Herring, saying that Smith was "of a temper and disposition fit for the office [provost of the college] . . . . and shall have my countenance and friendship— whenever that can be of service to him."

The details of the agreement between Penn and Smith were in a large packet of letters and papers which Smith sent to Franklin and Peters, and which were lost at sea. In a letter which has survived, Smith says, "The proprietor was not at first satisfied that such liberal institutions were useful to an infant country. Your academy also interfered with a design he had in view of his own, and of which he intended to be the founder. These and many other circumstances were obstacles. But when I was able to show the worthy gentleman the necessity of such a seminary in a political light, he generously agreed to ingraft his scheme upon yours. . . ." Penn agreed to the founding of the institution and to Smith as its provost. He also agreed to give substantial money to the college and to add £50 a year to whatever salary Smith got from the board of trustees.

Horace Wemyss Smith, biographer and greatgrandson of William Smith, owned a diary by his forefather which has since been lost. Indeed, it is likely that Horace, who wanted William to be remembered at his best, lost or burnt more than one stack of papers. From the diary he extracted and preserved two entries for the end of December, 1753:

> 26th. Started to the North, to see my honored father.
> 31st. Preached in the kirk in which I was baptised.

What a glory it must have been for Smith! Raised in poverty and doing, until he was twenty-three, nothing to suggest that he would not live all his life in poverty and obscurity: a grammar school teacher, an occasional contributor to little magazines, a lay reader, perhaps, in some country chapel; he returned at twenty-six, freshly ordained by the Bishop of London. Suddenly, he was the intimate of Benjamin Franklin, of Thomas Penn, of Peter Collinson, of the Archbishop of Canterbury, who—as Smith said in a letter and as he undoubtedly said more than once in person—"has been very kind to me. I have seen him oft and he said he would provide for me." Smith was declining the provision only because of "the precariousness of the Archbishop's life, as he is in a very bad state of health."

It is unlikely that Archbishop Herring could have done much for Smith in England, where the only preachers who cut a figure in the world were those who came to the pulpit with money or aristocratic connections. But in America, where there was little money and no aristocracy, a preacher stood out as a man of education and refinement, a natural choice as a leader. Even a college degree (or, in Smith's case, the pretension to one) gave entry to the best circles in America, and to a chance for distinction. Naturally, there were preachers who missed that chance, but Smith wasn't one of them.

When he returned to Scotland, he had become not only a dignitary of the church but also a famous author: his "Brief Account of the Academy in the City of Philadelphia" was in the current issue of *Gentleman's Magazine,* and his books were being published on both sides of the Atlantic. He was soon to be provost of a college. His wages, in three years, and allowing for the discrepancy between English and Pennsylvania currency, had increased at least tenfold. His bearing and manners, which he was always adjusting to suit the importance of his audience, must have shown some changes too, and not toward humility. And the text of his sermon—well, it has not survived, and perhaps it is best left to our imaginations. "Blessed are the meek?"

Smith arrived in Philadelphia late in May, 1754, almost exactly a year after he had left it, better than three months of that year having been spent in getting across the ocean and back. Three days later, the minutes of the trustees of the Academy noted that Mr. Franklin and Mr. Peters were to speak to Smith, in case he would undertake to teach logic, rhetoric, ethics, and natural philosophy. Evidently, he would.

# 2 ✿ Politics

Smith started work at once. For the time being he was only a teacher, and his superior was the rector, Francis Alison, a conservative but humane classical scholar. He had had ten years' experience running a Presbyterian school in Chester county, south of Philadelphia.

"I have many more acquaintances than I can possible pay due civilities to, consistent with my duties to the college, which you may be sure neither preaching nor company shall divert me from," Smith wrote to Thomas Penn a year later. "I have not preached since Christmas, and cannot find time to compose anything this way in such a manner as I would choose to address the public. When my first course of lectures is finished I shall have more leisure, as all afterwards will be little more than repetition of the same subjects."

In addition to teaching, Smith initiated a system of periodic public exercises at the Academy. These exercises usually consisted of verse prologue and epilogue, framing a series of orations spoken by the students, though Smith supervised the composition of them. The exercises emphasized the students' ability to think originally on a variety of subjects; and although we are now used to faster entertainments, they were well attended in Philadelphia for many years.

Smith and Alison drew up a charter for the new college early in 1755. Smith was to be provost, although "I think Mr. Alison qualified for any station in any college," and Alison vice-provost. These positions do not correspond to president and vice-president, or even to dean. The provost of the College of Philadelphia was just another professor, but with a slightly higher salary, on whom the Board of Trustees could depend to do its dirty work. Thus Smith, in addition to teaching, was expected to see to the repair of the fences at the Norristown farm owned by the College, but was not expected to make decisions on large matters. It was not by the title of his office but rather by the force of his ideas and personality that he came to dominate the board, and to control the destiny of the College.

Alison remained rector of the Academy. The charter was soon approved and recorded, and the College grew naturally out of the Academy, taking over the students who had learned all they could. It was always small (one hundred and forty-one pre-Revolutionary graduates), but its curriculum was a model of liberality compared to other American colleges like Harvard and Yale, whose curricula bore, until well into the nineteenth century, the same relation to education that language records do to foreign travel. The classics were taught in massive doses, but a place was made for mathematics, including trigonometry, and for physics, biology, botany, and modern literature and history. The emphasis was on fluency in English, rather than Latin and Greek.

It was not his curriculum but his overbearing manner that put people off with Smith. In 1756, when the college had been in existence a year, a special committee of the trustees had to be set up to examine Smith's teaching and conduct. His students defended him, and four of them wrote a letter saying that all who spoke against him were "unjust and malicious. . . . He never advanced any other principles, than what were warranted by our Standard Authors." Already it was difficult to separate Smith's teaching from his politicking, but he was exonerated by the trustees, and for the time being his provostship was secure.

He always inspired great love in his pupils, and he must have been a superb teacher. Perhaps the most attractive episode of his life was his bringing together a group of young men, fostering their friendship, and seeing them become the first literary and artistic circle America ever produced. Several of them were interesting figures, and two of them achieved real distinction:

Francis Hopkinson was the son of a rich Philadelphia lawyer. He was small, frail, and witty, with a head "not bigger than a large apple," according to John Adams. He had the gift of not taking himself seriously. In 1753, he was already a student at the Academy, and in 1757 he became the first graduate of the College. He was eventually admitted to the bar, and was a signer of the Declaration of Independence, Treasurer of Loans to the Continental Congress, and finally a federal judge.

Hopkinson could do anything. He wrote good prose and poetry ("The Battle of the Kegs"), played the harpsichord and the organ, composed ("My Days have been so Wondrous Free"), edited a hymnal. He drew and painted gracefully. He invented an improved quill for the harpsichord. He kept up a long scientific correspondence with Washington, Jefferson, and Franklin.

He designed the American flag and the great seal of New Jersey. He never ran for elective office, but he served in many appointive ones, and was a fluent political satirist and pamphleteer.

Benjamin West was born in Swarthmore, Pennsylvania, of Quaker parents. Early praised—and perhaps over-praised—for his artistic talent, at eighteen he was making a living by it, limning portraits in Lancaster. There Smith found him and, by offering him education and a chance for further commissions, drew him to Philadelphia, where he remained three years. The rest of West's long life is well known: he studied in Rome and went on to London, where he became a member of the Royal Academy and historical painter to George III. His "Death of Wolfe," which showed the general and his adjutants in uniforms rather than togas, horrified the king and the public; but later it established West's reputation as an innovator, which—by any artistic standard—he was not. He was always generous to young American artists in London, and several generations of them learned and bummed from him, including the Peales, Stuart, Trumbull, Allston, Sully, and Morse.

In the curriculum he established for West, Smith showed to the fullest the flexibility of his mind. West was too old and his formal education had been too long neglected for him to become a regular student of the Academy or College, so Smith gave him the classics in translation and, as West later described it to his biographer, "Directed his attention to those incidents which were likely to interest his fancy, and to furnish him at some future time with subjects for the easel. He carried him immediately to those passages of ancient history which make the most lasting impression on the imagination of the regular-bred scholar, and described the picturesque circumstances of the transactions with a minuteness of detail that would have been superfluous to a general student." Smith also got him commissions, had him study whatever pictures and engravings were available in Philadelphia, and urged him to go to Rome, where he could learn from the best. In 1760 Smith persuaded William Allen, who was sending a grain ship to Italy, to give West passage.

Thomas Godfrey, the poet, was the son of Thomas Godfrey, who invented "Hadley's" quadrant well in advance of Hadley himself, and was eventually given an award by the Royal Academy, though Hadley got the patent. Before the birth of the poet, the Godfrey family boarded with the frugal Franklin, but left when Franklin declined to marry one of their relatives, even though she was "very deserving." The elder Godfrey was, with Franklin, a founder of the Junto, the Library Company, and the American Philosophical Society. In addition to his skills as a glazier (he glazed Independence Hall), mathematician, and astronomer, he was a notorious drunk; but his son did not live long enough to master even one discipline: poetry.

Godfrey the younger at first aspired to be a painter; thwarted in that, he moped for a time and then took up poetry as a pleasant and inconspicuous diversion from his trade as watchmaker's apprentice. He had no connection with the Academy, and probably no formal education, beyond what the Germans of Germantown may have provided him; but in 1757 he sent —anonymously—quite a finished little poem to Smith's *American Magazine*. Smith praised it and printed it, and when subsequent submissions revealed Godfrey's identity, Smith wrote that with only "an attentive perusal of the works of Dryden, Pope, and one or two more English poets, [he] has exhibited such proofs of poetical capacity as really surprize us."

Smith at once introduced him to his other protégés. Relieved of his apprenticeship and commissioned an ensign in the army, Godfrey continued to write poetry. Later, he went as a grain factor to North Carolina, wrote the first American play ever produced, *The Prince of Parthia,* and died—apparently of heat prostration—at twenty-six.

*The Prince of Parthia* is composed in the iambic pentameter that hamstrung the theater until long after Godfrey's day. Its royal characters and lofty motives, like those of Dryden's *Aurengezebe* and Shakespeare's *King Lear,* owe only their inspiration to history. There are occasional good lines, as in one song:

> Youth in pleasure should be spent,
> Age will come, we'll then repent.

but in general, the versification is only competent, and not equal to his better lyric poetry. It must have taken Godfrey a lot of long, muggy Carolina evenings to write it.

Jacob Duché was, like Hopkinson, a student at the Academy when Smith began teaching there. After graduating from the College, he studied further with Smith, went to England and took orders, and returned to become Richard Peters's assistant and successor at Christ Church and St. Peter's. He married Hopkinson's sister.

Duché wrote pleasant, undistinguished prose and poetry, but he was a supremely likeable young man. "His disposition to laughter was natural to him," says Benjamin Rush, "so much so that he was obliged when a young man to pinch himself in the pulpit to prevent his laughing when he was preaching." Rush also says that he changed his religious opinions often, but "was under all these changes truly amiable, pious, and just." Duché came a cropper in the Revolution. He was at first a patriot, and was made chaplain of the Continental Congress; but when Howe captured Philadelphia and incarcerated him, he wrote a letter to Washington, urging him to sue for peace. His friends—even Hopkinson—turned against him, for in the heat of battle they could not allow him the weakness of his character. He fled to England and did not return—a Swedenborgian—until he was an old man, in 1792. By then the battle had cooled, and he was "kindly received by all his old friends."

Nathaniel Evans was the youngest of the group, so much so (in 1757, Godfrey was twenty-one, Hopkinson and Duché were twenty, West was nineteen, and Evans was fifteen) that he may have been more of a tag-along than a companion. However, he was for many years a student of the Academy and College, and his eighteenth-century schoolmates, who did not make such nice chronological distinctions as are now the fashion, may have recognized his ability and accepted him as an equal.

After six years at the Academy, Evans was withdrawn by his parents and apprenticed to a businessman. But, says Smith, "He devoted more of his time to the service of the muses than to the business of the counting-house," and he eventually returned to the College. Evans was a poet, and "on account of his great merit and promising genius," in 1765 he was awarded a master's degree, though he had not yet received a bachelor's. He then went to England to take orders and returned to preach in Gloucester county, New Jersey, where he died of tuberculosis at twenty-five. In 1772, Smith collected and published his poetry.

Evans himself had performed the same sad office for Godfrey, adding a preface, in which he made some sharp observations: "Considered purely in a political sense, the works of genius are, of all others, the cheapest entertainments." Evans's own poetry is imitative in form and content: odes, eclogues, epistles, songs. Some is humorous, without meaning to be so: "To Benjamin Franklin, Esq., L.L.D., Occasioned by hearing him play on the Armonica." In some, the humor is deliberate:

> How happy is the country parson's lot?
> Forgetting Bishops, as by them forgot;
> Tranquil of spirit, with an easy mind,
> To all his vestry's votes he sits resigned:
> Of manners gentle, and of temper even,
> He jogs his flocks, with easy pace, to heaven.

Evans still holds a place in some anthologies of American verse. Had he lived, he would probably have developed as a preacher and let his poetry slide.

The circle—Hopkinson, West, Godfrey, Duché, Evans, and occasional others, such as the future general and president (governor) of Pennsylvania Joseph Reed, for the circle was not wholly exclusive—the circle that Smith nurtured spent a great deal of time goofing off. Philadelphia in 1757 did not cover half the two square miles William Penn had set aside for it, and often the young men tramped to the banks of the Schuylkill, which was still the clear, clean, "hidden river," full of islands and sandbars, that it had been when the Dutch named it. "Many of Godfrey's verses were composed under a clump of pines which grew near the upper

ferry of the river Schuylkill," West related, sixty years
later. The whole gang of them liked to go fishing there.
In the heat of the day, Godfrey "used to stretch himself
beneath the shade of the trees, and repeat to them his
verses as he composed them." That is not far from the printer Keimer, whom
Franklin, on his first visit to Philadelphia, discovered
composing an elegy straight from the type case. Godfrey
may have been vain enough to have simulated spon-
taneity for the edification of his friends, but more likely
West, who was sedulous in sponsoring myths about his
own beginnings, kindly decided to do the same honor
to his departed companion. At any rate, Godfrey's poetry is infinitely better than Keimer's, and its finished
form can only result from that inevitable poetic process,
thought and erasure.

How oft together Schuylkill's verdant side
We've traced, or wantoned in its cooling tide,
Or soft reclined, where spreading shades were wove,
With joyful accents filled the sounding grove.

A. F. Gegenheimer, in a literary appreciation of
Smith, points out, "The simultaneous production, by
three friends, of the first American musical composition
[Hopkinson], the first American drama to be profes-
sionally performed [Godfrey], and the first American
painting of permanent worth [West], is a phenomenon
that invites inquiry." Gegenheimer gives a large part of
the credit to Smith, and undoubtedly he is due it: he
brought them together, he prompted their efforts, and
he was in many ways their model.

It is most interesting of all that this first artistic
circle, this first American intelligentsia, should have
seen society at large in the same terms as did all other

intelligentsia that followed it. Society was boorish; society was stupid; society was best run away from, to the banks of the Schuylkill where the intelligentsia could privately, exclusively, intelligently fish and skinny dip. West, on coming to Philadelphia, was at once introduced by Smith to "four other young men, pupils of his own, whom he particularly recommended to his acquaintance, as possessing endowments of mind greatly superior to the common standard of mankind." Thus were the American muses launched on their long—and perhaps requisite—career of suspicion and alienation.

*The American Magazine, or Monthly Chronicle* was published by Smith as a vehicle for himself and his pupils, beginning in October, 1757. The lead article, usually on politics in one form or another (an analysis of the American Indian, or of European affairs), was followed by a "Philosophical Miscellany," a group of short articles on a number of subjects, including the aurora borealis, sea monsters, geometry and calculus problems, eclipses of Jupiter's satellites, recipes for bread and stew, the natural history of Iceland, and yaws. Next came the "Monthly Essays," including two serials: "The Planter" by "Agricola," which appeared in every issue, and "The Hermit," which appeared in about half the issues, sometimes by and sometimes about a figmentary pastoral recluse who was given to lamenting human vanity. There were three to five pages of poetry, and three to five pages of chronicles from other colonies and abroad.

The last number, published as "a supplement to volume 1," contained an index to all thirteen numbers. Its "Philosophical Miscellany" was entirely given over to Smith's "Account of the College and Academy of Philadelphia." It had to be the last number because

Smith, who wrote about half the magazine and edited the whole, had to go to England to appeal his conviction of having libeled Assembly.

The salient virtue of *American Magazine* was that it did not, like other colonial periodicals, devote most of its space to advertising and the rest to shipping news. As a result, it was a financial success at one shilling a copy, and it may well have been the best magazine published in America before the Revolution. Nonetheless, it told very little of what was happening in Philadelphia, because its patrons were assumed to know that already, through handbills, gossip, and their own senses. The magazine printed the poems of Hopkinson and Godfrey, and of other, less talented Philadelphians as well. "Upon seeing the portrait of Miss _____ by Mr. West" (probably Hopkinson's work, though few of the poems were signed) was the first recognition West was given in print. The "Philosophical Miscellany" reflected the breadth of a mind in no way inferior to Franklin's, though it turned out to be on the wrong side of political history.

Smith had not been in Philadelphia long before he realized the similarity of his opinions and Richard Peters's, even though Smith was flamboyant and Peters was retiring. Peters came to Pennsylvania in 1735, fleeing the embarrassment to himself and his second wife when it was discovered that his supposedly dead first wife (a household servant with whom he had had a youthful liaison) was very much alive. He was a qualified lawyer and preacher, and he became James Logan's lieutenant and successor in managing the affairs of the Penn family. He later became rector of Christ Church and St. Peter's. He was one of the original members of the Academy's board of trustees, and in 1756 succeeded Franklin as president of the board of the Academy and College. He got along with Franklin until he discovered that he could get along even better with Smith. However, the shock of his romantic disappointment, and the ensuing publicity, had made him a far less combative man than Smith, and he got into far less trouble.

Smith's private interests and his politics kept him so busy that, according to Dr. Rush, he could usually be found "Anywhere but at the College." His first political enemies in Pennsylvania were the German sectarians and the Quakers, who allied to control Assembly and would not vote any money for war with the dispossessed Indians, or even for the more dangerous war with the French. Smith was writing against the Germans before he took up residence in Philadelphia, and the Quakers came in for their licking soon after. "I hope," he wrote to Thomas Penn as early as November, 1755, "you will support every step that shall be taken for their exclusion from Assembly." Earlier, his "Brief State of the Province of Pennsylvania," published in London, had urged that English be the only legal language (invalidating German wills), that Assembly members be required to speak English, that printing in foreign languages be restricted, and that Assemblymen take a test oath which would effectively exclude pacifists.

When copies of this pamphlet went on sale in Philadelphia, Smith was tickled to see that they "made a prodigious noise in this city. Frequent consultations of Friends have been held last week, and it is said that they were never known to be so vexed before." Like most of his political writing, he did not sign the pamphlet, and he claimed that rewards were being offered for the identity of the author. But most people soon concluded that he was the author, because no one else was enjoying the stir as much as he was.

Smith's ambitions were three: for the College, for Pennsylvania, and for himself. Contrary to what his enemies thought, he probably never did hope to see the College a church institution. He spoke often of liberty, and as a member of a minority he had reason to mean it. However, he did hope to see the Church of England dominant in the College, and also in Pennsylvania as a whole. Once they had control, the Anglicans could dispense toleration on the old country model, because only *they* could be trusted as guardians of everyone's liberties. There were limits, of course, to how far toleration could extend (as in Britain, where papists had no franchise), and Smith believed that a toleration as broad as William Penn's was mere license.

In Pennsylvania, the struggle was not simply between the Quaker and German pacifists on one hand and the city merchants and expansionist frontiersmen on the other. Franklin, for example, was a city merchant who leaned so far toward the Quakers that he eventually became their agent; and many German quietists lived on the frontier. There were also Presbyterians of two varieties (though Francis Alison united them finally) whose politics were in some ways distinct. And there were many other interests, among them those of the proprietors, who were represented by the governor (by the nature of his job) and by William Smith (by his own inclination). The proprietors wanted the land they were stealing from the Indians to be protected for them by the citizenry; and even when they paid fair prices, all occupied lands were stolen and potentially troublesome because the Indians could not conceive of private property, and could not imagine that they were selling anything more than the right to joint use to their white friends.

The proprietors also wanted to collect their quit-rents but be exempt from real estate taxes on their own holdings, for they still owned most of the province. Assembly wouldn't defend their property until they paid some taxes, and maybe after that it still wouldn't. The governor was giving the Penns representation without taxation, said Assembly.

The problem for Smith and the Penns—and many other aristocrats and would-be aristocrats have faced it —was to find a way to disenfranchise the majority, while preserving the illusion of representative government. In the spring of 1756 Smith wrote a letter to the London *Evening Advertiser* attacking Assembly, and escaped prosecution for it only because Assembly resolved that, more important business being at hand, "further proceedings in relation to the said Smith, be postponed to a more convenient opportunity."

The attack in the *Advertiser* was not the first time Smith's politicking had gotten him into trouble. Six months earlier, he had earned a letter in the *Journal* by "Humphrey Scourge." Scourge, masked as a French agent, claimed that Smith was a Jesuit, and said, "Our very worthy Friends the Proprietors of that province have already seen the service this Father is like to be to their and our designs, and have therefore settled a pension upon him."

Beyond his "pension," which he did have, Smith hoped to become a bishop, the first Anglican bishop of the New World. There was a distinct need for one in America because, by an anomaly of Anglican lore that still exists, a mere preacher may baptize but may not confirm. It was a modest enough ambition except that

Smith also hoped to see the church established in America, as it was in England. He would then have become a second Archbishop of Canterbury-across-the-pond. So obvious were his intentions that Humphrey Scourge, now masked as a Quaker, dealt with them at length in a letter to the *Journal* in March, 1756:

MILD ADVICE TO A CERTAIN PARSON

Friend

I perceive thee art extremely busy in many matters, some of them not pertaining to the duty of thy calling, and others of mischievous tendency. . . . Do not, my friend, for the sake of pleasing a few small grandees, offend God and thine own conscience, and get a bad name among the peaceable and discreet. Indeed, thee wilt find that the favor of the Great Ones is no inheritance; but, 'tis said, thee expects by their means to be made Bishop of America; and that thee has already begun to try thy hand at pastoral letters. . . .

I have before me a book that quoteth a Latin passage from the Christian Constitutions, that were written, it is said, by the apostles themselves, and containing some cautions and rules for a bishop; the same I send, in love, for thy perusal. I send also the translation, to save thee trouble. . . .

And now methinks I hear thee reading them, and venting thine own observations in soliloquy, viz, *Let a bishop not be fond of making his court for gain.* Pray what else should he make it for? *Let him not be contentious in his station.* Not *contentious!* Why so, I pray? Here is certainly a syllable or two too much; read it content. . . .

Some people thought that Scourge was Benjamin Franklin, but more likely he was Franklin's son, William, who was then clerk of Assembly and who had good reason to think that in harassing Smith he was defending his father. The Indians, prodded by the French, were becoming increasingly self-righteous along the frontier, which extended roughly from Allentown to Reading. Franklin went up to build forts, and it was generally conceded that he would be elected colonel of the Philadelphia militia on his return. Smith called a meeting in the Academy building to organize an "independent militia"—that is, independent of Assembly and Franklin. When Franklin got back, he found that there were two militias, and he and Smith harangued each other in Bradford's *Journal* (*not* Franklin's *Gazette*).

As soon as an independent militia was proposed, Smith said, Franklin "took alarm, marshalled his host, and in due form marched up with great guns, and ponderous axes, and fierce steeds, and lighted matches, and all the dreadful apparatus of war, to lay seige to—*a poor half sheet of paper.*" One of Franklin's friends (not Scourge, whoever he was; he had too much wit) undertook to answer for him: "The vomitings of this infamous hireling . . . betoken the redundancy of rancor, and rottenness of heart, which render him the most despicable of his species."

Within the year, Smith had the poor taste to respond in figures almost as repulsive. And he saw to it that, in June, 1756, the trustees of the Academy and College made Richard Peters their president, bypassing the incumbent Franklin. "The church, by soft and easy means, daily gains ground" in the college, he wrote cheerfully to Thomas Penn. And when the *American Magazine* came out, it was of course printed by Bradford, not by Franklin and Hall.

Really, Smith was a fantastically busy man. His lectures, which he had expected to become "little more than repetition" after the first year, cannot have done so, with a whole college curriculum superimposed on the Academy and Smith in charge of much of it. He directed the periodic public exercises of the College and Academy, and the production of a full-length play in January, 1757. He did sometimes find time to preach, and to involve himself in church—as well as Pennsylvania—politics. In May, he organized the first commencement of the College, awarding Bachelors of Arts to eight students, including Hopkinson, Duché, and Josiah Martin, the surviving one of the brothers Smith had tutored on Long Island. He visited Huntingdon on the Juniata (where he was later to establish his own proprietorship) and other towns more or less on the frontier, to advise them about setting up schools. He interested himself in educating and proselytizing the Indians, and even in having some of them as students in the Academy. He was also still working, though without much success, for the Society for Propagating Christian Knowledge among the Germans. We do not know where he ate and slept during that period, but he must have slept very little.

The only rest he had in 1756–57 may well have been the few hours he spent having his portrait taken by West. The picture has been "restored" so often that it is no longer a reliable indication of what Smith looked like at the age of 30; but fortunately, John Sartain engraved it in the nineteenth century, and on the engraving we now depend.

It shows a man still young, though beginning to be jowly, with strong features, heavy eyebrows, and a very large forehead. He stands with his right hand pointing oratorically and his left hand on an open book, the topmost one of a pile. He wears a clerical robe, but the intention is to show him both as preacher and as teacher, and he looks to be confident of himself in both capacities—or in any other, for that matter. It is the portrait of a leader, by a painter who had every reason to admire him.

In August, 1757, Smith made his first land purchase: seven acres at the Falls of Schuylkill, on both sides of Ridge Avenue and including riverfront, for which he paid £71/5/0 at auction. Perhaps it was intended as a speculation, but he never sold this land: it became the nucleus of his enormous holdings on both sides of the river at the Falls, and the site of "Smith's Folly," a house he intended for his country seat. It became, in the years of his decline and disgrace, his sole residence.

In September, 1757, Assembly conducted an investigation into charges by various citizens against William Moore, Justice of the Peace and presiding judge of the Chester county court. Moore appeared and claimed that he was not cognizable to Assembly, but Assembly nonetheless decided that he had committed several kinds of extortion, "wickedly and corruptly through an avaricious disposition and designedly to oppress and distress the poor inhabitants." It asked Governor Denny to remove him from office, and the Governor said he would look into it.

Moore next appeared before a session of the Governor's Council and, reading from a prepared statement, said that the charges against him were scandalous, and were trumped up by "one of the members or rather tools of the late Assembly, through the most unjustifiable practices, many of them at a tavern. . . ." The whole thing was "a standing monument to scurrility and abuse." Moore was so pleased with his statement that he had it printed in as many newspapers as would take it, including a German one that his friend William Smith found for him.

Assembly had adjourned, and when a newly elected Assembly convened, in January, it decided to forget about the Governor's investigation and charge Moore and Smith with publishing a "seditious libel." Thus it happened that, on the day of the Governor's hearing, the defendant was unable to appear because, five days earlier, he and Smith had been arrested and clapped into prison.

Moore and Smith were tried by Assembly, and both pleaded not guilty, Moore saying that libel cases were to be heard in court, not in the legislature; and Smith that it was all Moore's fault, and that anyway, an election having intervened, this wasn't the same Assembly as the libeled one. Although Smith was much less guilty than Moore, and less guilty than many others in the case, Assembly had it in for him, because most Assemblymen believed that he had written the piece and given it to Moore to sign, and both he and Moore were convicted. Smith was offered an opportunity to recant, but he refused, and all those in the gallery who applauded him were arrested and fined. His request of an appeal was refused, and he and Moore were sent off to the "Newgate or common jail of the . . . county, the place for thieves, murderers, and felons, as well as debtors, there to be detained until further orders from the House." The sheriff was ordered that "he do not obey any writ of *habeas corpus* or other writ whatsoever, that may come into his hands for bailing or discharging the said William Smith."

Smith and Moore remained in jail until April,

when Assembly adjourned and they were freed. The Governor, with Council, then heard the Moore malfeasance charges and their defense, and in August exonerated Moore entirely. It is likely that this judgment was correct, and that the charges were trumped up by Moore's Quaker enemies in Assembly. However, by that time libel was the main issue, not malfeasance.

During the four months Smith spent in jail in 1758, his activity in no way diminished. His students strolled over from the College (it was only a block or two away), and he taught them as he would have in the classroom. He brought out an issue of *American Magazine* every month. He helped organize a lottery to raise money for his College. And, for the first time that we know of, he wrote love poetry:

> What means this change, that revels in my breast;
> Fills all my soul, and robs me of my rest? . . .

In June, two months after his release from his first term in jail, Smith was married to Rebecca, daughter of William Moore, at Moore Hall in Chester county.

Nothing is more revealing of Smith's rise in the world than his marriage. Jonathan Swift describes the matrimonial prospects of an English preacher: in his advice to a lady's maid, he says, "If you happen to be young with child by my Lord, you must take up with the Chaplain." The prospects of a parochial schoolmaster cannot have been much different; but in Pennsylvania, four years after taking up residence, and still with little capital about him beyond his own wits and bearing, Smith was married to the daughter of one of the richest men in the province. What made it even better was that it was a marriage for love as well as for convenience.

Everyone who knew Mrs. Smith—even her husband's detractors—liked her and spoke well of her. As
painted by West in 1758, she is blonde and sprightly
looking, wearing a satin and lace dress and blue rib-
bons in her hair. She has, at twenty-six, a rather round
face, but so do all West's portraits of that period.
Strangely, she is holding in her left hand a lemon well
past its prime.

From his behavior in public life, it is hard to imagine William Smith having a conjugal and affectionate
nature; but evidently he did. He and his wife went on
having children until she was forty-three, and they
probably went on trying for a good while after that.
His letters to her were warm and thoughtful, and there
is no suggestion that he ever looked at another woman,
even during his fund raising trips, one of which lasted
two and a half years. She was always "my dear wife" and
"the heavenly woman," and she seems to have borne
with him as he did with her, making an unusually
happy marriage.

Soon after the wedding, Smith saw that he would
have to recant to Assembly, or spend the rest of his life
in jail, or go to England to pursue his appeal. The appeal had been made from jail in January; but Benjamin Franklin, who was now in England as agent for Assembly, was of course doing all he could to block it.
Assembly had issued a new warrant for Smith's arrest
late in April, but it had never been served. In September, a third warrant was issued, and Smith spent most
of that month under arrest. Taking a final swat at
Franklin in the last issue of *American Magazine*
(Franklin "has not been careful enough to distinguish
between" his electrical discoveries and other people's),
he sailed for England in December, 1758.

# 3 &#10087; Falls of Schuylkill

"He has no charge as a clergyman. His character as such, or as a schoolmaster, was not now to be hurt, by the censure of the house for publishing a libel, he having been long considered as a common scribbler of libels and false abusive papers against public bodies and private persons, and thereby keeping up party heats in the province. . . . The place of his confinement is in a separate building from the criminals where only debtors are confined, in airy commodious apartments, where confinement is the only inconvenience. . . . Smith is an old offender, and was formerly treated with great lenity by the Assembly on a like occasion. He receives a pension from the proprietaries of £50 a year, as provost of the Academy and being a ready scribbler is employed in all the dirty work of abusing and libelling the Assembly. . . . It is a matter of not sufficient importance for the King in Council to be troubled with."

So Benjamin Franklin, in a passage that his admirers do not often quote, assessed William Smith's appeal to Privy Council. The gist of Franklin's arguments was that whether or not Smith had committed any offense, he was a rotter and better off rotting in jail. For Franklin it was the only possible argument, because everyone knew that his own paper, the *Pennsylvania Gazette,* had printed Moore's libel of Assembly long before Smith had had it printed in the German paper.

Smith, just out of jail in Pennsylvania, was not able to be in London to defend himself against Franklin; but Thomas Penn's lawyers did what they could for him, and he also had common sense on his side. Franklin, seeing that he was likely to lose the case, tried to postpone the judgment, so that Smith could enjoy for a little longer his "airy, commodious apartment, where confinement is the only inconvenience." Franklin cannot have been pleased when, on New Year's Day, 1759, William Smith arrived in London.

Smith did not immediately petition the Attorney-General. His friend Archbishop Herring was now dead (vindicating Smith's prediction), but Secker, the new Archbishop, was also a friend, and with a little politicking Smith got him and five other bishops to write to Oxford, recommending Smith for a Doctor of Divinity degree. The letter described Smith's quarrel with Assembly; in fact, it made it the strongest reason for conferring the degree upon him. The degree was conferred late in March; two weeks earlier, and presumably by a similar process, Smith picked up another honorary D.D. from his alma mater, Aberdeen. At the time, Oxford was thinking of giving Franklin a degree too; but Smith, who was now an alumnus, wrote a letter saying that he was unfit for it, and Franklin had to wait until 1762 for his honor from Oxford.

Smith also saw to the printing of his *Discourses on Several Occasions,* which, said the *Monthly Review,* "show the value of the blessings arising from the enjoy-

ment of the protestant religion and civil liberty."
Franklin bought a copy and wrote a piece of abusive
doggerel in the flyleaf.

In April, Franklin confided to his Philadelphia
partner David Hall, who was home minding the store,
"Parson Smith has been applying to Osborne for a large
cargo of books, acquainting him that he could be of
vast service in selling great quantities for him, as there
was only one Hall at Philadelphia who demanded excessive prices; and if another shop was but opened
where people could be supplied reasonably, all the custom would run to it. I know not whether he was to sell
them himself or employ some other. [Hall, who was
selling books to support Franklin, must have enjoyed
that gibe.] He gave Osborne a catalogue. Osborne came
to me, and asked me if I knew him, and that he should
be safe in trusting him. I told him I believed my towns-
men who were Smith's creditors would be glad to see
him come back with a cargo of any kind, as they might
have some chance of being paid out of it."

Though Franklin's main interest was in eliminat-
ing a potential rival who was better read than he and
Hall put together, there was some justice to his saying
that Smith did not pay his bills. William—son of James
—Logan wrote to a potential landlord of Smith's, "He
is accounted so very bad a pay master that it may be difficult for thee to get thy rent from him." And Dr.
Rush, in his summation of Smith's life, said, "He seldom paid a debt without being sued or without a quarrel."

Bad pay master or not, Smith won his appeal to
the King on July 26. Privy Council ruled that Moore's
libel was a libel, but only against the 1757 Assembly,
and that no future Assembly had the right to proceed

against him or Smith for it. Council was incensed that
Assembly should have ordered the sheriff to disregard
royal writs of *habeas corpus,* and that Assembly should
have taken to itself the dignities and powers appropri-
ate to Parliament alone. It suggested that Smith's false
arrest and incarceration were grounds for a damage
suit; but Smith had triumphed enough, and he never
did sue Assembly. He sailed for home a few weeks later.

Smith had good reason to be fervent in his appeal:
his liberty was at stake. The reason for Franklin's fervor appears in a letter he wrote about a month after
Privy Council's decision: "Before I left Philadelphia,
everything to be done in the Academy was privately
preconcerted in a cabal without my knowledge or par-
ticipation. . . . The trustees have reaped the full advantage of my head, hand, heart, and purse, in getting
through the first difficulties of the design, and when
they thought they could do without me, they laid me
aside."

Both sides in the case acted mainly from personal
motives, but Smith and Moore were supported by
principles—free speech and due process—which were
fashionable then and have become more fashionable
since; while Franklin's and Assembly's principle—
oppression of the individual to preserve the dignity of
the state—was going out of fashion even then. To
Smith's credit, he quickly grasped the public implica-
tions of his private quarrels: as early as March, 1756, he
was asking Franklin in the *Journal,* "Whether Englishmen had not a right to meet and consult together?
. . ." By the time he got to England, he had achieved
real eloquence: "Hard, indeed, would it be if there
could be *right without remedy,* and if a body of men in
any part of his Majesty's Dominions could range at

pleasure through the wide Fields of Oppression in any part of Majesty's Dominions, in that old abolished Star Chamber manner, banishing, persecuting, and imprisoning his best subjects from year to year, without jury or any known process of law, and no relief within our constitution."

Henry Bouquet, the Swiss-born English army officer quartered in Philadelphia, wrote happily, "Provost Smith is expected in Philadelphia, having defeated the Philistines completely." Smith was reunited with his wife, and had a chance to see his first child, William Moore Smith, who had been born in June. He returned at once to teaching at the college, but for the next few years he did less politicking, and devoted most of his time to education, the church, and his private interests.

He brought with him the deed to one quarter of the Penn's Manor of Perkasie (a manor was land that the Penns held for speculation after selling off the other ground round about. Perkasie Manor was four square miles). By the agreement of 1754, now fulfilled, Thomas Penn was giving land to the College, and at the same time ending the £50 "pension" that had so often figured in the newspapers. It was a couple of years before Smith could persuade the trustees that he was entitled to that extra £50 from the rents of the manor.

Horace Wemyss Smith says that his great-grandfather started building his house at the Falls of Schuylkill soon after he bought his first parcel of land there, in August, 1757. However, it is unlikely that Smith had the money to start building until after his marriage, ten months later; and as he left for England six months after that, the house may not have been started until after his return, in October, 1759. At any rate, a Sunday stroller noted it in her diary for June, 1762, so it must have been nearly completed by then.

The Falls of Schuylkill was a picturesque spot before the Fairmount Dam put it under water in the beginning of the nineteenth century. The river, varying in width from one hundred to two hundred yards, flowed in a gorge from Conshohocken to the Falls, between wooded hills a good two hundred feet high. There were numerous cataracts in this straight, six-mile course, the last and most impressive being the Falls, below which the river was tidal. From the east side (Smith's side) a long, flat rock projected most of the way across the stream. According to a contemporary of Smith's, it formed "a complete natural dam, a part of it overhanging on the lower side. In high freshets the water flowed over it and made a beautiful cascade; at other times it forced the water into a narrow channel on the western side, through which it ran with great rapidity and much noise, falling some five or six feet." On a day when the wind was right, its roar could be heard in the city, five miles away.

Almost from the beginning, the Schuylkill had been navigated by lumber rafts. Later, scows of as much as twelve tons burden came downriver in flood season. At Manayunk, and also at the Falls, people gathered on the hillsides to watch and cheer the Reading boats as they shot the rapids. At other seasons, they gathered to catch herring, shad, perch, and rockfish, and especially migrating catfish, for which the Falls became famous. By 1760 there were three "fishing companies," which were really gentlemen's gastronomy clubs, near the Falls, and there were two mills using the power of the Falls Run, which debouched in the river just above the great rock.

Smith built his house on a knoll near Falls Run and halfway up the hillside, from which he had a view for several miles to south and northwest, showing long stretches of the river in both directions, and a nearer view of the Falls itself. The valley he looked out over had more cleared land than it does today (cemeteries and Fairmount Park have supplanted farmlands), and more morning mists, and the constant noise of roaring water. The house itself was unpretentious, and the wings and outbuildings that Smith was forever adding made the place quaint, rather than handsome. At least one bay, unusual at the time but part of the earliest construction, soon earned the place—with all its outbuildings—the collective name of "Smith's Octagon" or "Smith's Folly" or "Plush Hill." William Smith, however, is not known to have called it anything but "my house at the Falls."

In 1879, Horace Wemyss Smith boasted that he was still living in the house, and that his young grandson was the sixth generation of Smiths to live in it; but forty years later it had run down and was out of the family hands. Several of the outbuildings were razed, and the main house was eventually cut up into apartments. Today, a tract of several acres remains; but the Roosevelt Expressway, soaring on concrete and steel to span the Schuylkill, looks down on it from a few hundred feet away, and the original planting has given way to stinkweed and scrub, and the house itself was razed in 1965.

Smith was hardly back in Philadelphia before he flung himself into the Macclanechan controversy. William Macclanechan, an Irish Presbyterian-turned-Anglican, who had recently quit a New England parish and even more recently signed onto a Virginia one, found himself in Philadelphia in the spring of 1759 and was invited to preach at Christ Church. Dr. Jenney, the rector, was old and paralytic, and Mr. Sturgeon, his assistant, was overworked because he had to catechize blacks and whites separately, and because the congregation was burgeoning as more and more burghers discovered the advantages of the Church of England. The vestry had requested that Jacob Duché be made another assistant; but the Bishop of London—within whose see Philadelphia fell, in spite of the curvature of the earth —had not yet replied.

Macclanechan preached. As Smith later described it, "The novelty of his manner, his great noise and extempore effusions, both in praying and in preaching, struck sundry of the lower sort of people. . . . He addressed the Majesty of heaven with a long catalogue of epithets, such as 'Sin-pardoning, all-seeing, heart-searching, rein-trying God.'—'*We thank thee that we are all here today and not in hell*'— Such an unusual manner in our church sufficiently fixed my attention. . . . I have heard him again and again, and still we have the same wild incoherent rapsodies, of which I can give no account, other than that they consist of a continual ringing of changes upon the words regeneration, instantaneous conversion, imputed righteousness, the new birth, etc."

Many of the congregation decided they wanted him as assistant, or at least as a lecturer. Jenney agreed to allow him the pulpit, though at Jenney's own pleasure, as a lecturer only, and "not withstanding my known dislike to the man." The ruckus started when, a few months later, a majority of the vestry named Macclanechan a permanent assistant and wrote to the Bishop of London, requesting that he approve their action.

There is no record of how the majority of the parishioners felt (it wouldn't have mattered anyhow, in an episcopacy), but the Anglican clergy of Philadelphia united behind Jenney, drew up a remonstrance against Macclanechan, and sent it to the Bishop of London on the same boat with the vestry's request. In November, Smith sent a long letter to Secker, describing the whole affair as well as Macclanechan's manner.

It was eight months before the reply came, refusing Macclanechan a license and telling him to return to his flock in Virginia. In that time, Jenney had first required him to conform to the Anglican prayerbook (which was latitudinous enough, God knows) and, when that failed, had excluded him from the pulpit. Macclanechan set up his own church in a room that Assembly made available to him in the State House (Independence Hall), and there he preached, he claimed, "to above, perhaps, five thousand hearers." Though Smith advised Secker that Macclanechan's followers were only a few "tools of the Quaker Party," there were in fact enough of them to build him a separate church, where he preached for several years before moving on again. The Archbishop thanked Smith for his report, but said, "You will see that there are two or three small chronological mistakes in it. And all mistakes should be avoided, but especially all exaggerations, in speaking of an opposer. Such things give him great advantages." Poor Smith! had he followed that kindly advice, both then and in the future, what a world of trouble he would have spared himself!

Of the affair there remains one incident, and that reported only by Horace Wemyss Smith, who was at least as given to mistakes and exaggerations as his great-grandfather. Still, it may have happened: at a convention of Anglican preachers, attended by Macclanechan and chaired by Smith, a complimentary address was written to the Bishop of London and signed by all. Later, a letter was read which implied that the Bishop would deny Macclanechan his license, and Macclanechan said he then wanted to erase his signature from the address. He was refused, but he jumped up and grabbed the paper. Smith grappled with him, pinioned one of his arms to his body, and wrestled the paper out of his hands, while the other preachers looked on. It was all done as quickly and neatly as if, "at Mr. Macclanechan's request, Dr. Smith had been adjusting a sleeve-button." Smith resumed the chair and continued the meeting as if nothing had happened.

Whether or not he did wrestle with Macclanechan, the convention did take place on April 30, 1760, and was attended by the active Anglican preachers of Philadelphia—Smith, Jenney, Sturgeon, Duché, and Macclanechan—and by missionaries from Pennsylvania, Delaware and New Jersey. Addresses were prepared, especially one to Archbishop Secker, which requested a bishop for North America, so that confirmation and ordination could be had without a trip to England. As Smith pointed out in the dedication sermon of St. Peter's, even a building could not be consecrated without a bishop to do it. The address, however, did not state *who* should be Bishop of North America.

Smith took an interest in the missions, which were under the care of his old friends, the Society for the Propagation of the Gospel, and were administered—somewhat erratically—from London. A mission was, to the society, not necessarily an organ for converting the heathen, but more likely a church with too small a congregation to support a preacher. The society then subsidized the preacher, to prevent scattered Anglicans from sliding off into Methodism and other abominations. Much information about the pre-Revolutionary frontier all up and down the eastern seaboard comes from the letters these missionaries wrote back to the society.

In August, Smith went to Reading, to preach and to encourage the Anglicans there to appeal for a missionary. He made many such trips into the hinterland to give advice and encouragement about education and religion, and it is impossible to chronicle them now, though one does occasionally come to light. The trips served a number of purposes: they made him known, looking forward to the day when he would aspire to offices in church and state, and would need a host of adherents. They acquainted him with the land, and no doubt even then, with his wife's dowry weighing his pocket, he was considering land speculations on a scale he had not dreamed of three years earlier. And also, they expressed his very genuine interest in the growth of education and the maintenance of his religion. It is doubtful that these trips ever paid him expenses, but he is never known to have refused one; and in 1765 he took over and for some years conducted a small, unprofitable parish in northeast Philadelphia County, from which he got little or no money, nor information, nor —as it turned out—adherents.

In 1760, the College commencement was held May 1, the day after Dr. Smith is said to have pinioned Mr. Macclanechan. Eight B.A.'s were conferred, and M.A.'s were given to Hopkinson, Duché, and the other members of the class of '57. In that day (and at Oxford and Cambridge even today) the M.A. was awarded to all who had held a B.A. for three years and came to apply for it. The commencement of 1760 might mark the end of Smith's group, though the camaraderie of it had

*William Smith at thirty by John Sartain after Benjamin West*

*William Smith at Seventy-five by David Edwin after Gilbert Stuart*

probably been in decline for several years. Duché was now a professor of oratory at the College (as well as assistant at Christ Church), and Hopkinson had no connection with the College at all. West was in New York, and soon to leave for Italy. Godfrey was in North Carolina. He had sent his *Prince of Parthia* to Smith in the fall of 1759, but it had arrived too near the end of the theater season for Smith to get it produced that year, and in fact it was not produced until four years after Godfrey died.

Smith never formed such a group again, and never published another magazine. There were many intelligent and interested students in the College: Evans was there until 1765, Thomas Mifflin graduated in 1760; Thomas—brother of Francis—Hopkinson, Tench Tilghman, General John Peter Muhlenberg, and William White all studied there in the early sixties. Smith continued a "perspicuous and agreeable" teacher, but he no longer inspired his pupils as he once had; and although they admired him in some ways, they no longer adored him.

Alcohol is seldom attractive to the young, and an adult who uses it heavily is to them a member of a different and unintelligible species, whom they do not necessarily shun, but from whom they prefer to keep a certain distance. His smell is disagreeable to their keen nostrils; his tousled hair and rumpled clothes are at odds with their pride in their own young bodies. They had rather stay clear of his belches and his farts, his jibes and non sequiturs, his uncertain gait and unpredictable gestures.

Smith's drinking in his later years was a matter of such common knowledge that even Horace Wemyss Smith has to admit that he might once have "transcended the limits allowable to the clergy." The truth is far more dramatic: Ezra Stiles calls him a "contemptible, drunken character," and even the more charitable Benjamin Rush says, "He early contracted a love for strong drink, and became towards the close of his life an habitual drunkard. He was often seen to reel, and once to fall, in the streets of Philadelphia. His temper was irritable in the highest degree, and when angry he swore in the most extravagant manner."

Rush credits Smith's penchant for liquor to the rough characters with whom he lived on his land speculation trips. Rush was a teetotaler, and to him alcohol was a contagious disease, not a self-generating entertainment. However, it seems more likely that Smith—a Scot, remember—always liked the good taste of liquor, that he bought it as soon as he could afford it, that from the time of his marriage he regularly drank as much of it as he thought he could handle, and that he was sometimes mistaken in his calculations. Many other people have done it, and in spite of falling down once in a while they have lived long and useful lives, though seldom in close intimacy with young people. Drunken he may have been, as Stiles says, but he was not contemptible on that account, or on any other.

There are much more serious charges to be made against Smith and his institution. First, it fostered a hazing system, on the good old English model. Alexander Graydon, who was enrolled for six years, beginning in 1760, was forced to fight an older, stronger boy to prove that he was worthy "of the name of an Academy boy." There was a whole system of chivvying and harassment, inflicted by the bigger boys upon the smaller, by the older boys upon the newer, which could have survived only with the tacit approval of the faculty.

Second, the curriculum and the manner in which it was taught bored most students so much that they lived for nothing but to play pranks on the teachers, and left without taking degrees. Most descriptions of the Academy and College were written by administrators, who give us a favorable—if somewhat abstract—picture; but Graydon in his *Memoirs* gives us what sounds like a wholly different institution. Whether in the English or the Latin school (and Graydon had his fill of both), the teaching was uninspired and repetitious. "At length, with a single exception, we became possessed of the demons of liberty and idleness: we cheerfully renounced the learned professions for the sake of the supposed liberty that would be the consequence. . . . I was thoroughly tired of books and confinement." Graydon did not stay to enter the College. He—a man of unusual literary interests and ability—must have given it a fairer try than most students did; and although no school in eighteenth century England or America was any more inspiring, there are limits to the praise that should be heaped on the Academy and College of Philadelphia.

The education might have been better if Smith had spent more of his time at the College; but he was too busy with other things. In the summer of 1760, he was politicking to be named to the commission surveying the Delaware-Pennsylvania boundary (a tricky business, because the line is the arc of a circle, twelve miles in radius, with its center at New Castle). He was not appointed, though he was qualified, and served on similar commissions later on.

In November Thomas Duncan Smith, his second son, was born. The following spring, Smith bought twenty-six acres adjoining the seven acres on which he was building his house at the Falls of Schuylkill, and before the year was out he had bought a total of ninety-four acres on the opposite side of the river. Eventually, he came to own most of Belmont Plateau, though he sold one hundred and forty-one acres of it to John—son of Richard—Penn in 1773. Land was not his only interest at the Falls: in January, 1760, Thomas Penn sent him a patent—which he must have asked for while still in England—granting him exclusive ferry rights. It came just in time: some months earlier, a Phineas Roberts had petitioned the court to allow him a road to the ferry he had already built at the Falls. With Smith's urging, the court refused him, saying, "The petitioner has not any settled or established ferry over the River Schuylkill, as by the said petition is falsely insinuated."

Smith's patent was good for seven years, and was renewable, and it guaranteed him no competition for a mile in either direction. His ferry consisted of a wharf on either shore, a flatboat big enough to carry a team and wagon, a rope strung from shore to shore to keep the boat from drifting downstream, and a man to pole or paddle or pull the rope, as the mood struck him. At the same time that he secured his ferriage, Smith secured confirmation of a new road, Indian Queen Lane, which started at the ferry, crossed Ridge Avenue, passed near the site of his house, and went on up the hill to Germantown. At the intersection of Ridge Avenue and Indian Queen Lane he built the Falls Tavern, which he leased out to a Mrs. Blackwood in 1763. He also owned fishing rights along the river, and leased them out, too.

Before he left for England, in January, 1762, Smith took the first steps toward acquiring eight hundred acres in Huntingdon; while he was gone, Richard Peters completed the purchase for him.

Some time before he left, he joined the Mount Regale Fishing Company, whose members (gentlemen all, including the Governor of the province) liked to gather at the Falls to do a little fishing and a good deal of eating and drinking. They had a clubhouse, and an awninged bateau on the river, and Madeira of two grades, and a steward to watch over it and them. One summer evening, they went through "Beefsteaks, 6 chickens, 1 ham, 1 breast veal, 2 tongues, 2 chicken pies, 1 quarter lamb, 2 sheep's heads, peas, salad, radishes, cream cheese, gooseberry pies, strawberries, 2 gallons spirits and 25 lemons."

Smith was also a member, and at various times president, of the St. Andrew's Society, whose purpose was to help fellow Scots get started in the New World. The meetings of the society, however, came to be more and more like the meetings of the Mount Regale Fishing Company, until the more staid members passed a by-law in 1765 forbidding any further feasts. In addition, Smith was a Freemason from at least 1755 onward, and probably from before he came to America. The records of the Pennsylvania Grand Lodge are missing for the sixties and seventies, but no doubt Smith was active there, as he was everywhere else.

By the fall of 1761, Smith had convinced the trustees of the Academy and College that he should be sent to England once again, this time to solicit an endowment for the College. Since its founding, the College had run a deficit of nearly £1000 a year, which had been made up by public lotteries; but the Quakers had often objected on moral grounds, and had several times gotten bills through Assembly to prohibit lotteries. Each time, the governor or the crown had vetoed the bills, but the feeling remained that lotteries were not really respectable, and that a subscribed endowment would do more to guarantee the stability of the institution.

As on his last trip, Smith's place at the College was to be temporarily taken by John Ewing, a young Presbyterian preacher and protégé of Alison's, who was later to take Smith's place in a more permanent way. In their letter of instruction to Smith, the trustees said, "If Mr. Franklin should be in England on your arrival, we desire you will wait upon him . . . and we doubt not but he will readily advise and assist you, and by his means you may be recommended to many persons of wealth and distinction." How could the "cabal" have been so sure of that?

Smith left for New York in January and for England a month later. Once again, his wife was pregnant, and there was no possibility of her accompanying him on a winter crossing. Smith preached, a few days before he set off, the funeral sermon of Dr. Jenney, but we cannot be sure that he had the time to influence the vestry in the choice of a successor to what was still the only Anglican church in Philadelphia. There were several possible candidates, but Duché was unlikely because he was so young, and was not even ordained until a trip to England later in the year. Sturgeon had been an assistant for twenty-three years, but he didn't have the social connections necessary to a rector, especially as he had for so many years consorted with the black parishioners. Macclanechan was still in town, and no doubt he would have accepted the rectorship, because it was Jenney's failing health that had made him try so hard for the assistantship two years before. For that matter, the vestry could have chosen any one of the missionaries, or even a preacher from another colony: Jenney himself had come to Christ Church from Hempstead, Long Island.

The vestry's choice was Richard Peters, who had recently resigned as Provincial Secretary. Peters had been an assistant at Christ Church when he had first come to America, in 1736–37, but had quarreled with the rector, been smeared as a Methodist, and forced to withdraw. It was now twenty-five years since he had worked at his principal trade, but he liked the idea of it, and he had made enough money with the proprietors to be able to do what he liked. It would be remarkable if Smith, his avowed friend and the most prominent Anglican in the city, did not have a hand in promoting his selection.

# 4 ❀ The Last of England

Smith arrived in London March 18, 1762. He must have had an uncomfortable crossing because, when he began thinking of returning to America, he wrote, "I will by no means take a winter passage." His first stop must certainly have been the house—a modest one—of his brother Charles, who had moved to the city and become a stationer. He may have seen Thomas Penn the day of his arrival; the next day, the 19th, he waited on Archbishop Secker.

Smith had with him a formal plea from the trustees "to all charitable persons and patrons of useful knowledge" in England, and with it he hoped to gain admission to the houses of the rich, collect £20 to £50 at a crack, and in a short time bag the whole four or five thousand pounds (a pound sterling was, at the time, worth almost two pounds Pennsylvania currency, because Pennsylvania—like other colonies—had for some time been printing paper money). Secker told him that a royal brief (ordering all Church of England preachers to dun their parishioners for contributions) would only net him about £1000 because the device had been overused lately, and Smith was that much more determined to solicit privately. On March 26, he made an example of Thomas and Richard Penn by getting £500 from them.

Smith also called on Benjamin Franklin—his letter of instruction from the trustees required it. It may have been an unpleasant interview, but Franklin did agree to give Smith a list of names, and to recommend the cause to his friends. He could not do more, he said, because he was soon to return to Philadelphia; and besides, he had the gout. Smith set to work, and contributions began coming in—the early ones mostly from ecclesiastics—and it seemed that all might go well; but Franklin went down to Oxford the end of April to receive an honorary degree, and while there he learned of the letter Smith had written three years before, which had prevented his getting the degree at that time. Franklin took it "in great dudgeon," said Smith, and immediately began advising his friends not to contribute to the College. To a dissenter, he said that it was all but closed to dissenters, and to an Anglican that it was "an instrument of dissension." To all he said that the College didn't really need the money anyway, and could perfectly well get it from Assembly if it did.

Smith was some time discovering why doors were shut to him, because he did not at first understand that Franklin had lost the ability to distinguish between him and the College, and that the old man would as soon strike at one as the other. When he found out, he countered as best he could: to dissenters, he showed a letter from Francis Alison; to Anglicans, he spoke of his own church connections. He spread the news that Franklin's popularity was declining in Philadelphia, which made Franklin so mad that he denied it at least four times in his correspondence, twice to the same person. However, Smith was right: two years later, Franklin lost his Assembly seat.

Unfortunately, the letter Smith wrote to Oxford in 1759 has not survived. That it was derogatory, even Smith admitted, "Though as we stood then, and his doing all he could to support Assembly in oppression and prevent my obtaining redress, he could not expect that I could say anything in his favor." With William Strahan, Franklin's friend and fellow printer, acting as go-between, Franklin and Smith met at Strahan's; but, said Smith, "explaining did not mend the matter much on either side." According to Strahan, Smith retracted much of what the letter said, and promised to write Franklin a letter of correction. He never wrote that second letter, says Strahan, and when asked why not, he pretended he had never made any such promise, and that his original letter needed no correction.

It is a sorry business for anyone who would like to admire Franklin, and even more so for those who would like to admire Smith. Strahan's account is probably correct, because Smith, in writing to Peters, says, "If he [Franklin] says nothing about the Oxford letter, I would not have you say anything." Smith's rancor had taken him too far and, unwilling to admit that he had behaved badly, he did not scruple to give his word and retract it, to lie, to sweep it all under the rug. It is another instance of the behavior which, all his life, made better men than Franklin avoid him.

By July 10, Smith had collected £725. On that day, he was visited by Dr. James Jay of New York, who told him that he had come to England to solicit money for Columbia, and that he expected to get a royal brief for the purpose. "I am so disconcerted that I know not what to do," wrote poor Smith who, whatever his faults of character, was genuinely devoted to his College. On his way through New York, he had told people he was going to England to raise money; and the New Yorkers, thinking about it after he left, had decided that it was a good enough idea to imitate. If Jay was applying for a brief, Smith would have to join him in a joint brief, with the two of them sharing the work and sharing the loot; otherwise it would seem that Philadelphia's appeal was less proper than New York's. A petition for the joint brief was drawn up and Smith and Jay sat waiting with it several days, until the queen was taken to bed and delivered of the prince who was to become George IV. Smith then flung on his best gown and rushed to court, where he found George III in a very good humor and ready to grant any petition. 11,500 briefs had then to be printed—one for every parish in England—and signed by Smith and Jay. It took a month and a half. In the meanwhile Smith collected another £260, two hundred of it from the king himself, who gave £400 to Columbia, perhaps because it was called King's College at the time, or perhaps because, as he said, the College of Philadelphia had the proprietors to look after it, but Columbia had no one but himself.

The middle of August, Franklin finally went down to Portsmouth to take ship. "He and I were not on the best of terms, nor the worst," said Smith. Smith was guarded about Franklin, but Franklin was virulently hostile to Smith, and became more so as time went on. "I have done with him," he wrote ten months later, "for I believe nobody will prevail upon me to give him another meeting." However, they did continue to meet whenever Franklin was in Philadelphia, because the city—the whole of America, for that matter—was not big enough to keep apart two men with interests so similar.

The quarrel between Smith and Franklin, which was really a collision of temperaments, has often been analyzed. The most usual conclusion is that Franklin, because he was so wise and famous and funny, must have been right. Another conclusion, equally wrong-headed, is presented by Horace Wemyss Smith: William Smith supported the Penns, but Franklin hoped to take Pennsylvania away "from a family ever beneficent to this province, and vest it in the government which so soon afterwards began to oppress us."

Franklin and Smith, who agreed so well when they first met, disagreed later because Franklin changed, not because Smith did. Smith's opinions and feelings, and even the phrases with which he expressed them, were fixed from the time he was twenty-five; but Franklin, when he retired from business as a middle-aged man, soon lost touch with many of the elements he had kept balanced in his printer's brain, and became what he was later to be officially titled, an agent of the Quaker-dominated Assembly. Soon after, Franklin ceased to be an American in everything but name.

Smith was born in Scotland, but after 1755 there was never any suggestion that he would return there permanently, because he had become an American. Franklin, after his first stay in England, 1758–62, was incurably a European. To Strahan, he said he meant to "settle here forever." To another, and writing from Portsmouth, he said, "I am going from the old world to the new; and I fancy I feel like those who are leaving this world for the next." And to Strahan, from Philadelphia in December, "In two years at farthest I hope to settle all my affairs in such a manner as that I may then

conveniently remove to England." Had he not gotten
the agencies and embassies that kept him in Europe
three quarters of the last thirty-two years of his life, he
would undoubtedly have settled in England long before
the Revolution. Small wonder he and Smith collided:
they were going in opposite directions.

A day or two after Franklin sailed for America, the
*London Chronicle* leaked the news that William Franklin, who was still in England, was to be appointed
Royal Governor of New Jersey. The appointment may
have been made to attach Benjamin Franklin even
closer to the royal interest, or it may have been simply
to secure a promising young man for a post that few
others would have cared to fill. William Franklin was
even less a friend of Smith's than was his father; and as
soon as Smith heard the news, he and Thomas Penn
conspired to have the appointment vacated by spreading abroad a piece of information that Benjamin Franklin had concealed during his four years in England:
the bastardy of William Franklin. The scheme was un-
successful: the appointment was approved. William
Franklin, of course, was enraged, and afterward spoke
of Smith as worse than the devil, and even as a "prosti-
tute writer."

It was not the first time Smith had tried to make
political capital out of William Franklin's birth,
though it loomed larger in London than it did in Philadelphia, where the circumstance was more usual. But
no matter how badly William Smith treated William
Franklin, he treated him better than his own father did
when—during the Revolution—the younger Franklin
remained loyal to the crown. Smith hated him with
real, human hatred; but his father felt nothing toward
him, nor toward any other human being, because he

had no human feelings, except lust and a twisted pride. That is why, for all Smith's human faults, our final sympathy in the Smith-Franklin quarrel must be with Smith.

Before Smith left London, the end of September, 1762, to begin his share of collecting for the two colleges, he must have learned of the birth of Williamina, his third child and first daughter, at Philadelphia, on the Fourth of July.

He and Jay divided up the country between them: Smith went north and Jay south, but they met in Oxford the end of November, issued a joint appeal, and raised £163, although "Dr. Franklin's friends were very averse." Smith went north again, traveling on horseback usually, covering many miles, speaking often, and getting donations of a guinea and half a guinea now, instead of twenty and fifty pounds. "You must be content with a very short letter by this packet," he wrote the trustees, "and it is well I am to write with my hands and not my feet, else you would have none at all." On the road as much as he was, he had very few opportunities to bathe; but bathing had never been a preoccupation of his. He never complained of the cold either, now that he was back home again, where good whisky was plentiful. Early in the new year he was joined in his solicitations by two young graduates of the college: John Morgan, who was in Scotland studying medicine, and Samuel Powel, who was making the grand tour. He wrote the trustees regularly, and deposited the money he had gathered to their account, and they wrote him not to think of coming home "one moment sooner than the expiration of the time limit of the brief," although "we are sorry you will be so long absent from your family."

At least once in his travels, Smith stopped to visit his Aberdeenshire family. "This act of duty I hope the Trustees will not think was throwing away their time." His father was now dead, but there were at home his stepmother, his sister Isabella, and at least two younger children. His brother Charles was in London; and Thomas, the eldest of the half brothers, had recently joined him there. A half sister, Jean, wanted to go down too, but Thomas would not allow it until he was better able to support and protect her. Thomas wanted to send money home, but at eighteen and without much education he was having a hard enough time keeping himself. The family continued genteel, but poor to the point of squalor.

William must indeed have seemed a creature from another world. He had audiences with the archbishop and the king, he was buying lands, he was building houses. He was undoubtedly generous with them: Thomas speaks of him as "my brother and benefactor," and in all his dealings with his family he was a different man from what he was with the rest of the world. But more than a handout, the family must have discussed the possibility of sending other Smiths to America to make their fortunes. Most of them did come, sooner or later, though Charles didn't like it and returned to London, and James was lost overboard, and Jean stayed home and took care of her mother, who lived to be nearly one hundred. But Isabella died at the Falls of Schuylkill in 1802, and Thomas came over in 1768, served as a colonel in the Revolution, and became a Pennsylvania Supreme Court Justice and a man whom many—including George Washington—preferred to his half brother William.

In March, 1763, James Jay was knighted, and in

April he and William Smith were together at Cambridge, where they collected £3 more than they had at Oxford, making about £3000 they had collected jointly. Jay, who had at first seemed "active and sensible," now began to seem a slacker, especially since his dubbing. "And then his address is not good, and he often stutters in speech, or speaks too fast to be understood—but still does as well as most laymen could in a business of this kind." Another problem was that Smith could not approach the middle class directly, because their own parish preachers did that through the brief; and the upper class was so badgered by petitioners and protected by servants that "you must call twenty times perhaps before the matter is finished." Still, he was doing well enough for the trustees to decide, in May, that he could come home whenever he thought best.

But the trustees, pressed for money, wanted to start spending the collection right away, rather than investing it for an endowment. Smith remonstrated, but some of it was spent anyway, and some of it was invested unwisely, so that Smith was very like the man who tries to pour sand into the neck of a sack quicker than it is running out the hole in the bottom. Searching for other ways to raise money, he canvassed dissenter as well as Church of England congregations, and prevailed upon David Garrick to lend him Drury Lane Theater for a benefit. In July he was in Birmingham and Liverpool, where many gave, but most gave less than a pound. Sometime that year, he got a chance to tell the Bishop of London what a good rector of Christ Church Richard Peters would make; and the bishop at length agreed, though he still thought Peters's two marriages a smelly business. Smith, in his letter to the Christ Church vestry in June, makes much of the Bishop's interest in having a separate see for the colonies, but again he does not speculate on who the bishop shall be.

In August, Smith took Samuel Powel to an audience with the king, who "kindly asked me some questions about our college and the success of our collection, and also received Mr. Inglis and Mr. Powel very graciously. I had almost got the latter dubbed a knight, but we thought it idle; and considered a design to separate him from his old friends the Quakers of Philadelphia." Smith had been gone a year and a half, but Pennsylvania squabbles were fresh in his mind.

He crossed to Ireland in September and fell sick there, but was nursed back to health by the Penns and "four score" of visits from a doctor, which—miraculously—did not kill him. He was awarded an honorary degree by the University of Dublin in January, and was able to collect another £600 before returning to England, from which he sailed for Philadelphia in April, 1764. His share of the money he and Jay had collected was almost £6000, and that, with the £1000 he had collected on his own, made about £12,000 Pennsylvania currency. That money, if reasonably invested, would have yielded enough income to offset the College's annual deficit; but it was frittered away, and fifteen years later there was not much left of it.

From Falmouth he wrote to his wife, "In a few hours I expect to be under sail in the *Halifax Packet,* a fine new ship; and I am happy in the hope of clasping you to my heart in a few weeks; and I am resolved that sea nor lands, nor any earthly circumstance shall ever separate between us again, till death comes and makes our separation final."

So much doubt had been voiced in England about what kind of institution the College of Philadelphia was becoming that Smith returned with letters to the Board of

Trustees from Archbishop Secker, Thomas Penn, and others, urging them to reaffirm the nonsectarian charter. The trustees did so, and all signed their names, and all agreed that all future trustees should be made to sign too. However, two thirds of the seats on the board continued to be filled by Anglicans, and the critics were not stilled.

Ezra Stiles, who later became president of Yale, hated Smith as much as any man living, and he found correspondents in Philadelphia to agree with him. "By supporting the College of Philadelphia, the flower of our youth are every day perverted by the intrigues of that designing subtile mortal, Dr. Smith," a Presbyterian wrote him. Even Francis Alison told him, "I am ready to resign my place in the College, and retire to the country merely through chagrin. The College is artfully got into the hands of Episcopal Trustees." For the fifteen years from his return from England until Assembly shut the doors of the College in 1779, Smith had his own way there. The trustees were agog at the money he had collected, and even William Allen praised his "prudence that I thought he used much to want." They voted him a guinea a day for the expenses of his trip, or about fifteen percent of what he had collected. They also voted him an annuity of £100 Pennsylvania currency, or about twenty percent of what their money would have yielded each year if wisely invested. Had he received his annuity until his death, he would have gotten back from the trustees most of the money that he collected.

Smith was now thirty-seven years old and had an income of £350 a year from the College and whatever else he could earn from preaching, surveying, etc. It was a pittance compared to what his wife brought him, but it still allowed him a measure of independence. He felt secure enough that July to write an introduction to a paper by John Dickenson which attacked Assembly and defended the proprietors. The answer, of course, came with an introduction by Benjamin Franklin.

In the fall, Franklin ran for reelection to Assembly on the "Old Ticket," as Philadelphia constituents then voted for slates rather than individuals. The campaign was bitter, but the "New Ticket" aimed most of its shot at Franklin, and narrowly won; and Franklin was without his Assembly seat. Nonetheless, his friends who did win were numerous enough to reappoint him agent to London. "New Ticket" Assemblymen protested, and were answered by Franklin in *Remarks on the Late Protest,* which in turn required Smith's *Answer to Mr. Franklin's Remarks.* Luckily, Franklin had taken ship by then, and there could be no *Remarks on the Answer to the Remarks.*

Even with Franklin gone, there were still plenty of writers eager to attack Smith and the College. In 1765 Isaac Hunt, a Barbadan who had graduated from the College two years earlier, published *A Humble Attempt at Scurrility; in Imitation of Those Great Masters of the Art, the Rev. Dr. S__th, the Rev. Dr. Al__n, the Rev. Mr. Ew_n_, the Irreverend D. J. D_ve, and the Heroic J__n D_____n, Esq.; . . . by Jack Retort, Student in Scurrility.* It was not Hunt's first essay in polemics: a year before he had attacked the Philadelphia Presbyterians, who also were partisans of the proprietors. Hunt was a royalist, insofar as he was anything more than a troublemaker.

Smith, Alison, Ewing, and Davidson managed to stay aloof from this fracas: the rebuttal was handled by David James Dove, a sometime English teacher at the

Academy and an almost full-time cartoonist and pamphleteer. Hunt was ready with a series of broadsides called *Exercises in Scurrility Hall*. When he applied for his master's in 1766, Smith and Alison made sure that he waited five years to get it, and gave it to him then only because Franklin, from England, intervened in his behalf. The degree, after all, was supposed to be automatic.

The College was enlarged in 1765 by the addition of a medical school, proposed by John Morgan, who had now completed his education and a grand tour and come home. Morgan, "with all his good parts, has given offense to many by being too desirous to put himself at the Head of Things," said Smith, who suffered from the same disease and knew the symptoms. Five years in Europe had also given Morgan more refined tastes than his fellow citizens; and he brought back with him several parasols, under which he and Jacob Duché disported themselves in the streets.

The medical school was the first in America. Morgan taught theory and practice—he was intent upon separating the branches of medicine, especially pharmacy, from each other—Edward Shippen taught anatomy and surgery, and Smith taught the related subjects of pneumatics, hydrostatics, and mechanics. Later, other teachers were added, including the young Benjamin Rush, who taught chemistry from 1768 onward; and by 1771 Smith was proud to say that his institution was "entitled not merely to the name of a College but of an University." A few—but very few—medical degrees were awarded before the Revolution.

In 1765, Smith wrote *An Historical Account of the Expedition against the Ohio Indians in the Year 1764. Under the Command of Henry Bouquet. . . .* "published from authentic documents by a Lover of his Country." He explains in the introduction that the conclusion of the Seven Years' War brought not peace but the most savage of all Indian uprisings, now known as Pontiac's Conspiracy, in which all the frontier forts but Detroit, Fort Niagara, and Fort Pitt were overwhelmed. The sieges of Detroit and Fort Niagara were raised with relative ease, because reinforcements could be brought in by boat; but Fort Pitt was relieved only after Smith's friend Bouquet, marching overland from Carlisle with four hundred men, fought a two-day battle with the Indians at Bushy Run, and suffered over one hundred casualties. Bouquet and his troops wintered at Pittsburgh.

The body of the *Account* describes Bouquet's expedition into the Ohio country the following year, where he subdued and made a tentative peace with the Senecas, Delawares, and Shawnees (the final peace could only be made by Sir William Johnson), and recovered many of the prisoners taken when the Indians had overrun smaller forts and frontier settlements. Two hundred and six prisoners were returned that fall, and more at Pittsburgh the following spring. Some had lived with the Indians ten years, and were loathe to return to civilization. "For the honor of humanity," says Smith in one of the few digressions he allows himself, "we would suppose those persons to have been of the lowest rank. . . . For, easy and unconstrained as the savage life is, certainly it could never be put in competition with the blessings of improved life and the light of religion. . . ." With the exception of the few who had actually made the comparison, Smith's contemporaries agreed with him.

The book was enormously popular: its audience

was the widest he ever achieved, and one edition followed another, in America and in London, Dublin, Paris, Amsterdam, etc. In 1870, it was superseded as history by Francis Parkman's *Conspiracy of Pontiac,* which was forced to draw heavily upon it, because Smith had given the most complete account of what Bouquet had said, and had talked with other officers of the expedition, including one who was a relative of his wife. Parkman's version improves on Smith's from Parkman's infinitely greater knowledge of Indian customs and character, and from the perspective of one hundred and five years, which allows him to place the expedition in the larger war; but Smith's is the better narrative: clearer, less conjectural, more circumstantial. He never wrote better, or with less bias (except, of course, that the relation implied the need of a stronger militia and a larger military budget). He did not sign it—he signed almost none of his writing, and neither did many other eighteenth-century writers—but he was proud of it, and sent copies to many of his friends.

The same year, Smith was hornswoggled by Alexander McNutt, a Scotch-Irish land promoter. Smith invested—as did his father-in-law William Moore, and even Benjamin Franklin—to give McNutt the capital to transport settlers to the twenty-seven hundred square miles he had been granted in Nova Scotia. The enthusiastic twenty-year-old Anthony Wayne was put in charge of the project; but when McNutt couldn't produce enough settlers and Wayne quarreled with Nova Scotian officials, the bubble burst, and the Philadelphia investors all lost. "Had I to live my life over again, I would never take up lands in partnership with anybody," Smith told Dr. Rush from his death bed. "This," said Rush indignantly, "appeared to be the only error he deplored in his conduct in the course of his long journey through life."

The next time Smith speculated in lands, he did it alone. The Standing Stone, or *Juniata* in the language of those who named it, was one of the great aboriginal landmarks of Pennsylvania. It stood at the confluence of the Juniata River and Standing Stone Creek, about 150 miles due west of Philadelphia. It was a monolith, perhaps carved with heiroglyphs, six inches square and fourteen feet high. It could be seen for quite a distance up the narrow river valley.

A subtribe of the Lenapes, who called themselves the People of the Standing Stone, lived near it and may have erected it. They were so convinced that their welfare depended upon the stone that when the Tuscaroras stole it, they fought a war to recapture it; and when their overlords, the Six Nations, signed away that part of Pennsylvania to the Penns in 1754 and forced them to migrate to Ohio, they took their fourteen-foot stone with them. In their wanderings, it was lost or mutilated beyond recognition, and so were they.

William Smith had, in 1762, secured warrants for eight hundred acres in several tracts along the Juniata River, and in 1765 he had bought eighteen hundred additional acres there. In 1766 he bought twenty-six hundred more, including the Standing Stone Tract of four hundred acres, which was sold to him by George Croghan, Sir William Johnson's deputy in the management of the affairs of the Six Nations, who had himself bought it from a Hugh Crawford, who may have run a trading post there in the days when the Lenapes were still about, and the stone still stood. Smith paid an average of four shillings an acre, but for the Standing Stone Tract he paid fifteen shillings an acre. As was his usual practice in land speculation, he did not take up first warrants, but bought from earlier owners who had already established clear title; and as he bought only choice lands, with river frontage or with agricultural or commercial potential (he knew the territory well, and had been there as early as 1756), the prices he paid were not excessive, even then.

As the lands east of the Susquehanna were nearly filled by 1766, and as the conclusion of the Seven Years' War and Bouquet's defeat of the Indians had made central Pennsylvania relatively safe for settlement, Smith laid out a town on the Standing Stone Tract in the winter of 1766–67. He chose the site because the Indians had already cleared much of it for their cornfields, because it offered several square miles of relatively flat land in a hilly country, and because it was already a known place to many Pennsylvanians. The printed deeds that he made up for the town lots call it "_____, at Standing Stone, on Juniata"; later, he named it Huntingdon, for reasons that no one seems now to know, though local historians have had a field day trying to find out. Until long after the Revolution, it was most often called by its original name.

Smith's town was to be a proprietorship. Each of the original town lots was to be sold for a quit or ground rent of one Spanish piece of eight a year. Had all sixty-three lots sold, they would have yielded Smith only about eight percent a year on his investment in the tract, an income he could have realized on a safer investment. The purpose of the town was not income, but an increase in the value of the surrounding acreage, most of which he owned.

The town did not build up immediately. It was a long way from civilization, and could be reached only by crossing mountains or by following the tortuous course of the Juniata, which was not navigable except in flood, and then at great peril. Huntingdon had only four or five houses at the time of the Revolution, but it was the center for a surprisingly large population of hillside farmers, most of them tenants or squatters on Smith's or Croghan's land. One Sunday in 1774, Smith baptized eighty children in Huntingdon, and it may have been on that day that he tricked one of his squatters in an incident recorded by Benjamin Rush. The squatter, on hearing that Smith had bought his property, declared that he would shoot him if he tried to make his title good by survey. Smith announced that he would preach, and when the squatter arrived to hear him, he sent men out the back way with transit and chain, and drew out the sermon until the job was completed. By that means and others, he eventually got clear title to seven thousand acres in the neighborhood.

Smith must have enjoyed his visits to Huntingdon. The frontiersmen were mostly immigrants like himself, and were mostly unscrupulous like himself, except that they were less successful at it. The earliest town records list at least four stills, and a man who lived there before the Revolution later wrote, "If any custom has been established among us by long usage and general practice, it is the deadly practice of drinking whiskey, which prevails among our whole community. . . . It was used when we were born, when we were buried; when we rose in the morning, when we went to bed at night; before dinner and after dinner; when we were hungry and when we were full; when we were sick and when we were well; when we were cold and when we were hot. It was the universal panacea."

# 5 ❧ The Transit of Venus

William Smith's real estate speculations brought him an acquaintance with George Croghan and Sir William Johnson. "It gives me great satisfaction to hear . . . . that you made kind inquiries after me and were pleased to remember me," Smith wrote in 1766, when he was hoping that Johnson would recommend him for a grant of land in upstate New York.

Sir William Johnson was the outstanding diplomat of America's colonial history. Born in Ireland, he settled on the Mohawk River above Albany and began taking up lands. His neighbors were largely Indians, whom he swindled in many a real estate deal; but he learned their languages and feelings so thoroughly that while still a young man he was adopted as a Mohawk. "Something in his natural temper responded to Indian ways," a friend wrote of him. His first mistress was a German, but he didn't make that mistake again; and before he died he had several dozen children of every conceivable color, most conspicuously the eight by Molly—sister of Chief Joseph—Brandt.

The Six Nations trusted him, and wanted no other

agent to deal with them, because he became one of them without renouncing his whiteness. He held them loyal to the crown in the French and Indian War, led armies of Indians and colonial militia in several battles, and was knighted for his military success in 1755. He was so much an Indian that he arbitrated quarrels between tribes, and so much a white man that William Smith—in spite of his fawning—genuinely admired him. He was instrumental in drawing the permanent boundary between Indian and white settlements in 1768—a solution that might have worked, had his white contemporaries been less rapacious than he.

In 1768, Smith was still wheedling Johnson for land. "Many persons have been favored in large grants of this kind. We want only a small one [12 or 15,000 acres]; and if you could yet help us to it in a good place or near anything of your own. . . ." Meanwhile, Smith had proposed Johnson for membership in the Society for the Propagation of the Gospel (in which—surprisingly—Johnson took an interest) and had gotten him elected to the American Philosophical Society. He enrolled Johnson's oldest son as a student at the Academy. Eventually Johnson did see to it that Smith got his land, and in his own county.

Smith worked with Johnson to strengthen the Church of England (which Johnson, with less circumspection than Smith, always called the *established* church) in the Mohawk Valley. To Johnson, the church was "the best support of monarchy," and he had no use for the New England missionaries proselytizing nearby, because they led the Indians to "neglect their hunting and worldly affairs." Smith thought that other Protestant sects might be allowed—"There is room for them and for us too"—and he sent Johnson an elaborate scheme, modeled after the Jesuit missions in Paraguay, which he claimed had the approval of George Croghan and Richard Peters. The Society for the Propagation of the Gospel was to set up two closed communities, each of a hundred square miles or so, and settle them with Indian and white families. Shielded from the world—there would be Society stores, as well as Society churches—the Indians could only imitate the whites and become Christians, especially the "rising generation of them."

Johnson read over the scheme, and answered, "None of the clergy of our church could submit to sacrifice their friends, hopes, and connections, to bury themselves in an obscure village." He also was able to foresee just how those rising Indians might arise. He had been a Mohawk for many years now, and he said, "Those Indians who have the least intercourse with us, have the most integrity and possess the best moral qualities." He asked instead that two teacher-missionaries be sent, whose students might someday go out among the tribes in an ever widening circle, to "convince their people of the advantages possessed by a civilized people, which from the mouths of Indians would receive double force."

Smith knew just the two men, though it must have galled him to swallow Johnson's dismissal of his plan. His plan for the College of Mirania had been thought out no more carefully, and it had brought him wealth and immediate position in the world. Almost from the day he landed in America, he considered himself an expert on Indian affairs, and an interpreter of them to less knowledgeable Europeans. Here is Smith at his worst: the study of their languages, which could have taught him much about a way of thinking different from his own, he never attempted. His extensive travels never took him beyond the frontiers, so that he never met an Indian who was not either an adversary or a sycophant. He did have a few Indians at the Academy, off and on; but from those bewildered children, who sat before him as students, not teachers, he did not take the trouble to learn anything. He was certain that they were merely white men manqué, except for that funny color their skins had, though that too might wash off with time and patience. A functional illiterate like Johnson, a religious enthusiast like Conrad Weiser, even a fool like William Penn understood the Indians better than Smith did.

Most of the lands Smith bought in his lifetime he bought from George Croghan, Johnson's deputy for Pennsylvania and Ohio. Croghan was as illiterate as Johnson: compare Croghan's "Pondiac and I is on extreame good terms," with Johnson's "I find yu. are displeased att my purchaseing the land, which in Everry Bodys Opinion is a good Bargain and Can any time I please Sell it for the Money and More So." He was almost as successful as Johnson: an Irishman who came to Pennsylvania in 1741 and went straight to the frontier, where he turned half native (the many Europeans who turned wholly native are seldom remembered by history). Croghan was at first a fur trader, but later an agent, and was once captured and tomahawked, "but my skull being pretty thick, the hatchet would not enter."

Huntingdon, for which Smith paid him £300, had cost Croghan £100 five years before. His investments moved westward with the frontier, and in his heyday centered around Pittsburgh, though he was—unlike Smith—a purchaser of first titles, on many of which he failed to make good his claim. He also bought land on credit, miscalculating how long it would take to appreciate. During the Revolution, nimble patriots smeared him with Toryism as an excuse to confiscate what remained of his lands, and when he died in Philadelphia in 1782 he was worth £52/13/6.

In the days when Smith knew him, Croghan was an extraordinary figure. He had a passion for everything: liquor, tobacco, women, promises. His word was worthless, but he loved fine clothes, crystal and china, and handsome houses as much as he loved Indian women and life in the woods. In addition to the Standing Stone Tract, Smith bought from him other lands on the Juniata, especially several tracts in Bedford county, one of which was the biggest single land deal Smith ever made. Their correspondence has not survived, and perhaps it is just as well; but Smith mentions him often in letters to other people, and the two of them must have known each other well, and understood each other perfectly.

In the beginning of 1768, the twenty-three-year-old Thomas Smith landed in Philadelphia. Like his half brother, who probably paid his passage, Thomas spoke with a thick Scottish accent, and cursed almost without thinking about it. Reading and writing were all his education, and only his relationship to William distinguished him from the thousands of other uncouth, poor, and pushy immigrants arriving in Pennsylvania every year. "Under that shaggy coat there was a kind and warm heart," says one who knew him. "His notions of ceremony were very strange, and with his utter inability to dress, or make a bow, or do anything else like other people, made him in some situations irresistable."

William intended that Thomas should help him

with his land speculations, and he apprenticed him to Surveyor-General John Lukens. Thomas and Lukens tracked through the back country, surveying lands that were being opened to settlement. They were in Huntingdon that year, and erected a new standing stone—this one only seven feet high—with their names and the date carved in it. This second stone had a shorter history than the first: within a hundred years, it was torn down in a "drunken melée," and pieces of it were used in the foundation of a house. The rough life he lived as a surveyor, though pleasant at the time, was sometimes an embarrassment to Thomas Smith later, when he had acquired more dignities. In the 1790's, when he was a circuit judge, he held court in a tavern in Huntingdon which had been partitioned off for the purpose. A crony from other days came around the partition carrying a punchbowl and saying, "Here, Tam, have a *bleer* o' this before ye charge the jury."

When new lands were purchased from the Indians in 1769, Smith was one of a dozen new deputy surveyors appointed by Lukens. William appeared to post bond for him at the land office and saw him set out for the part of Pennsylvania now included in Bedford, Somerset, Blair, and Cambria Counties. However, from a very early time Thomas Smith's interest seems to have centered around Bedford.

Bedford is a richer country than Huntingdon: broader valleys, higher hills. It drains to a northward-flowing branch of the Juniata, and is about forty miles southwest of Huntingdon. The Penn's proprietary manor of Bedford was the site of the town, which grew up around a fort, manned intermittently in the '50's and '60's, which was an important garrison on Bouquet's route. A good deal of the rest of the area was warranted to George Croghan, though William Smith had been buying a little acreage there since 1765. Smith didn't invest heavily in Bedford until Thomas was there to advise him; and he didn't begin to improve his holdings until 1771, when the war between the settlers (who didn't want guns sold to the Indians) and the traders (who did) calmed down, and Bedford became the seat of a new county.

Thomas Smith was the logical choice to be first county surveyor. Two years later, he was also prothonotary, clerk of the courts, recorder of deeds, and deputy register of wills. In 1774 he was made a justice of the peace, "with which office," says his usually stuffy biographer, "he seems to have absorbed a large part of the government of Bedford County." Most curious of all, in 1771, without ever having been admitted to the bar— and without having any qualifications which would entitle him to admission—he began to practice law. He never was admitted: his *readmission,* under the new state constitution of 1777, was automatically extended to him because he had been practicing under the old government. By that time, his clients included George Washington, whom he helped to evict squatters from lands farther west.

Thomas was an excellent agent for William in Bedford. He kept him apprised of tracts that were to be auctioned for taxes, and by 1778 William owned seven thousand acres in Bedford county, not to mention sixty-five hundred acres in Northampton and Northumberland counties, and about ten thousand acres in Tryon county, New York, and the seven thousand acres around Huntingdon. But Thomas, who remained honest and who did not marry money until 1782, had no means to become a land speculator himself, and perhaps no inclination either.

*Rebecca Moore Smith*
*by Benjamin West*

Courtesy of Williamina de Schauensee

*Thomas Smith,*
*brother of William Smith,*
*after a miniature by*
*an unknown artist*

*Williamina Smith,*
*after the miniature by*
*du Simitiere*

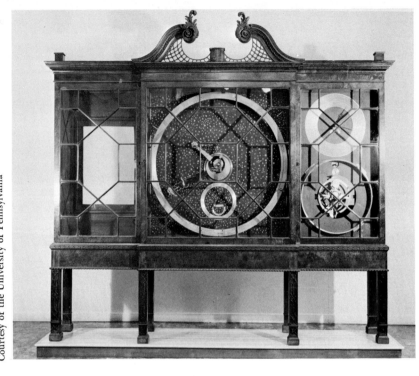

*above:*
*Rittenhouse Orrery*

*left:*
*Telescope built by*
*David Rittenhouse*
*to observe the Transit*
*of Venus, 1769*

Though William Smith was, from 1767 onward, more interested in real estate than in anything else, his great energy was not wholly spent in it. He continued active in the church, preaching fairly regularly at the mission he had taken on in northeast Philadelphia, and less often at Christ Church and St. Peter's. As his job with the College precluded his having a regular parish, he was a popular preacher to employ for special occasions, such as conventions and Masonic celebrations. In 1767, he helped found the Corporation for the Relief of Widows and Children of Clergymen in the Communion of the Church of England in America, which was modeled after a successful organization that Francis Alison and his fellow Presbyterians had put together several years before. Smith also continued active in the Masons, the American Philosophical Society, the Mt. Regale Fishing Company, the St. Andrew's Society, etc. All the while, he continued to teach at the College.

In 1767 the College, at Smith's instigation, awarded an honorary master's degree to David Rittenhouse. Smith had known about Rittenhouse at least since 1763, when they and a great many other men cooperated in the Pennsylvania-Maryland boundary dispute. The line was to run westward from the westernmost point of the twelve-mile circle around New Castle: a tricky problem in a rolling countryside. Smith, who was then in London, passed judgment on surveying instruments built especially for the purpose; and once the instruments arrived in America, they were taken to New Castle, where Rittenhouse was called to make "a number of tedious and intricate calculations." The surveying itself, which Smith had been so anxious to do, was finally given to Mason and Dixon, two Englishmen who were imported for the purpose.

Smith was introduced to Rittenhouse by Thomas

Barton, a preacher for the Society for the Propagation of the Gospel, who was also Rittenhouse's brother-in-law. Barton, fresh off the boat from Ireland, had opened a school near Norristown in 1751, and there he had found Rittenhouse, living on a farm, working as a clockmaker and nursing an ulcer. Rittenhouse was a tall, thin, highly nervous young man, and it is difficult today to see him as his contemporaries did: a magnificent scientist and idealist struggling against poor health. To us, Rittenhouse's hypochondria, his failure to achieve anything concrete, and his habit of collapsing at moments of stress invite psychological speculation. The eighteenth century was not psychological, and it considered him a "luminary."

With the aid of a few books, Rittenhouse had taught himself a surprising amount of science, particularly mathematics and astronomy; and Barton, who had had a college education, was able to give him advice and more books. Meanwhile, he supported himself with his clockmaking, got married, and dreamed of making his reputation with some scientific exploit that would set the world reeling. Such occasional employments as the Maryland border dispute must have been welcome diversions for him, but they were few and far between. At thirty-four, his prospects were hardly different from what they had been at nineteen, and the only outlet for his ingenuity was in making a clock so elaborate that it told the months, as well as the seconds, minutes, hours, and days; and it compensated automatically for leap years.

In 1767, Rittenhouse announced his intention to build the most elaborate orrery, or mechanical planetarium, the world had ever seen. When it was finally completed, in 1771, the center panel of the Rittenhouse orrery was four feet in diameter, and operated by a crank through clockwork gears. "By an easy motion of the hand," said Rittenhouse, "it will in the space of a few minutes, point out the time of all phenomena of the heavenly bodies for years to come." It had a separate clockface that told time from 4000 B.C. to 6000 A.D. by the Julian calendar, with a handset to correct to the Gregorian after 1752. The clockface was geared to the ivory planets Mercury, Venus, Earth, Mars, Jupiter, and Saturn, and their satellites: all the solar system then known, and all revolving around their own inclined axes and the gilt sun, in correct proportion to each other and in time with the clockface.

Rittenhouse said he had gotten the distances by his own calculations, "having never met with any that were exact enough for his purpose." By sighting through the sun and a planet to the outer rim of the orrery, the position of the planet in the sky could be told. To remain accurate through ten thousand years, the rim was geared to move one degree for every seventy-two years of orrery time. For simplicity of gearwork, only Venus had an elliptical orbit, and only Mercury changed speed during orbit. A side panel demonstrated eclipses of the sun and moon, and another showed an enlarged version of Jupiter and Saturn and their satellites. "He has not indeed made a world," said Thomas Jefferson, "but he has by imitation approached nearer its maker than any man who has lived from the creation to this day."

It was with a view to getting the orrery for Pennsylvania or, perhaps, even for the College of Philadelphia that William Smith gave the master's degree to Rittenhouse in 1767. Smith, who was one of the few Philadelphians with enough scientific knowledge to appreciate Rittenhouse's great potential, had decided that he was to be Rittenhouse's "discoverer," in the same way that he had been the discoverer of Godfrey and West, and had benefited both them and himself. He commissioned Rittenhouse to build him a clock and, with an imagination that few patrons of the arts possess, he specified that it was to have not six or eight hands but only one, because—as he said—his classes were an hour long, and the minutes until they were over were all that mattered to him.

The next step, after the degree, was to persuade Rittenhouse to move to the city. He had a secure living from the Norristown farm and the clockmaker's workshop, in both of which the burden of the work was done by the employees; he was needed there to direct both businesses, and was not about to leave until offered something better. By 1769, Smith thought he had it: trustee to Assembly's loan office, a £200 sinecure. The bill to create such trustees was defeated in a procedural bicker between governor and Assembly; and Smith did not convince Rittenhouse to move in expectation—rather than assurance—of preferment until the end of 1770.

Another reason that Smith was anxious to have Rittenhouse for his protégé was that he needed his help in observing the transit of Venus, predicted for Saturday, June 3, 1769. Great scientific excitement preceded the transit, which would not recur until 1874. Nevil Maskelyne, the astronomer royal, hoped that observations would be taken from as many different places as possible, and sent out instructions. He did not include Philadelphia in his plans because Benjamin Franklin, who knew that Smith would direct any observation here, advised him that nobody in the city was qualified or interested; but Thomas Penn sent a copy of the instructions to Smith.

The transit of Venus occurs when Venus passes between the earth and the sun. It appears as a black dot on the surface of the sun, and can be seen through smoked glass, with or without a telescope. If two observers at two exactly known points on Earth time the moment when Venus first appears to touch the sun, a comparison of the two times will, with computations and corrections, yield the sun's parallax, which means the angle described by two theoretical lines, one from the sun to the center of the earth, and the other from the sun to the outer edge of the earth. These two lines, and a third which is half the diameter of the earth, make a right triangle, with a known acute angle (the parallax) and a known side (half the diameter of the earth), from which the length of the other sides can be computed. As the orbiting times of all the planets are known, all of their distances from the sun can be computed—once the earth's distance from the sun is known—by Kepler's third law, which holds that the square of the orbiting time is proportional to the cube of the mean distance from the sun. For example:

$$\frac{Venus}{225^2} = \frac{Earth}{365^2} = \frac{Mars}{687^2}$$
$$\frac{225^2}{\text{distance from sun}^3} = \frac{365^2}{93,000,000^3} = \frac{687^2}{\text{distance from sun}^3}$$

The crucial information, then, for a knowledge of the whole solar system, is the parallax of the sun; but it is an angle so small (the twentieth century estimate is 8.8″, or about 1/409 of a degree) that a small error in timing or in measuring the distance between the two observation points will throw the calculation off by a good many million miles.

All over the world, governments set up committees to observe the transit. James Cook was sent to Tahiti for it, and the Royal Society sent another expedition to Hudson Bay. Numerous observatories were readied in England and throughout Europe, and even in Siberia and China. In Philadelphia, the American Philosophical Society appointed two committees to observe from two separate places, and a third committee was added later: one headed by John Ewing, Smith's sometime replacement as provost, to observe from the yard of the State House (Independence Hall); one headed by Smith, to observe from Rittenhouse's farm near Norristown; and one headed by Owen Biddle, to observe from Cape Henlopen. Assembly was asked for money, and gave a new telescope with micrometer and £100 for construction, most of which went to Ewing's group. Biddle got the Library Company's telescope, which was the finest instrument in the province. Smith got nothing.

However, Smith started with the best crew: apart from Ewing, the best astronomers in the province were Smith, Rittenhouse, and John Lukens. He wrote to Thomas Penn, and got from him a reflector telescope with micrometer, as good as the one Assembly had given Ewing. Rittenhouse built an observatory, a clock, an equal altitude instrument, a meridian telescope, and two refractor telescopes, the second one from lenses that were being shipped to Harvard via Philadelphia, and were quarantined here for the duration of the transit. Lukens borrowed an astronomical quadrant from the Surveyor-General of East Jersey, making the Norristown observatory at least as well equipped as the one at the State House.

"I am persuaded that the dependence which the learned world may place on any particular transit account, will be in proportion to the previous and subsequent care, which is found to have been taken in a series of accurate and well-conducted observations, for ascertaining the *going* of the time-pieces, fixing the latitude and longitude of the place of observations, etc.," wrote Smith. "And I am the more desirous to be particular in these points, in order to do justice to Mr. Rittenhouse." For months, while Lukens was busy with his surveying and Smith with his college, with his land speculations, and with seeing his wife through her sixth pregnancy, Rittenhouse was working toward the transit: timing the movements of Jupiter's satellites and shooting the sun with the equal altitude instrument to determine longitude; shooting the sun and stars with the astronomical quadrant to determine latitude; regulating and reregulating the clock, calculating the error (there was some) in the quadrant and the micrometer of the reflector telescope. When Smith and Lukens rode out to Norristown, on Thursday, June 1, they were rested, fresh, and eager; but Rittenhouse had worked himself into such a state of nerves that he was physically sick.

Thursday evening, after a week of clouds and rain, the sky cleared, said Smith, in "a state of serenity, splendor of sunshine, and purity of atmosphere," and continued so for the whole weekend. Saturday morning a crowd of yokels gathered around the observatory, and Smith lectured them to keep quiet, because the three observers, each with a telescope, were to signal silently to assistants the moment they thought the limb (edge) of Venus touched the limb of the sun, so that the three separate times could be compared. Smith was inside the building, which had a shuttered roof, looking through the big reflector telescope. It was capable of magnifications up to two hundred power, but he set it at ninety-five to keep his field of vision large because, at two o'clock in the afternoon, Venus would not be visible until the moment he was trying to record. Rittenhouse and Lukens lay on the ground outside, each with his head supported by an assistant, looking into the two refractors, which magnified to about one hundred and forty power. The hushed yokels stood some distance back. At the instant of contact, the burden of observing fell on Smith alone, because Lukens, whose telescope had a very narrow field, missed the first symptoms altogether; and Rittenhouse, when he saw the first symptoms, orgasmed and fainted.

Timing the transit of Venus is now discredited as a way of determining the solar parallax. The problems are two: the surface of the sun is a cloud of fiery gases, and it is impossible to say, no matter what smoked lenses are used, where its limb is. And the vapor clouds which surround Venus break up the sun's light, making a halo around the planet, which further obscures the point of contact. Exact timing is impossible.

Smith, Rittenhouse, and Lukens did not know that. The transit had been observed only twice before, and never before with such elaborate preparations for exactitude; and it could not be observed again for one hundred and five years. What they saw confused and disheartened them. "I was suddenly surprized," says Smith, "with something striking into it [the limb of the sun], like a watery pointed shadow, appearing to give a tremulous motion to all that part of the limb.

The idea I had formed of the contact was—that Venus would instantaneously make a well defined black and small impression or dent on the Sun. But this appearance was so different, the disturbance of the limb so ill defined, undulatory, pointed, waterish, and occupying a larger space than I expected, that I was held in a suspense of 5″ or 6″ to examine whether it might not be some skirt of a watery flying cloud."

As Venus progressed across the limb of the sun, it grew a tail of light behind it, and was soon entirely surrounded by a halo. When, twenty minutes after first contact, Venus should have been entirely within the sun, its silhouette lengthened in a "black drop" effect, as if the backwardmost part of its limb were stuck to the limb of the sun; and when the black drop broke, the planet was clearly well past its "second contact," which Maskelyne had been depending upon to be far more exact than the first.

What should they do? There was no telling how clear the weather was in other parts of the world, and how much would depend on their particular decision. Their reputations as astronomers would depend on it, certainly. They wrote down everything: the moment when they thought first contact occurred, with paragraphs to explain what they saw immediately before and after; the moment when it seemed that second contact occurred; the moment when the "black drop" broke. The two contact times, however, were clearly conjectural, and the breaking of the drop turned out to vary with different atmospheric conditions at different observation sites. Smith wrote sadly, "Some differences may well happen among the best observers, from their different manner of judging, in respect to a circumstance of such exquisite nicety." There was nothing left but to plot—as they did until nightfall—the course of Venus's transit across the sun.

There were other calculations to be made later: the distance between the Rittenhouse farm and the State House had to be exactly measured, which Smith and Lukens did in two days the next summer, tramping up and down Ridge Pike with transit, chain, and chain-bearers. Rittenhouse took further shots of the sun, and timings of Jupiter's satellites. Smith did the calculating, and using the data of ten different observation points he arrived at an angle of 8.6045″ for the parallax, compared to the accepted figure before the transit of 8.65″. However, he questioned the legitimacy of some of the data, and set to work on a new calculation, this time using only the Norristown observations and Maskelyne's observations from Greenwich. His final conclusion was that the parallax was 8.805″.

Although Smith was a better astronomer than most men who devote their lives to it, he was not primarily an astronomer, and his figure for the parallax was not accepted as the final word by astronomy books and nautical almanacs. Through much of the nineteenth century, 8.57″ was the accepted figure; and later it was supplanted by 8.93″. Today, by using radar, the accepted parallax has come to be 8.795″, a figure Smith missed by about one tenth of one percent.

Skulduggery accompanied the publication of the various reports. Biddle, who seems to have been an open and engaging man, though not a superb astronomer, gave his to the American Philosophical Society at its next meeting, June 16; but both Smith and Ewing said that theirs were not ready, and did not give them until the next month. Some members of the Society wanted all three sent to London for publication by the

Royal Society, but Smith convinced them that the proper place for the Philadelphia reports was in the first volume of the American Philosophical Society's *Transactions,* which came out eighteen months later. However, a nosy, ignorant Quaker sent Biddle's very sketchy report to Franklin right away, and Smith sent a copy of his very complete one to Thomas Penn; and both were published by the Royal Society a year before Ewing's report saw print. All in all, it was quite a triumph for Smith, though Rittenhouse wrote morosely to Barton, "The Doctor has constantly seemed so desirous of doing me justice in the whole affair, that I suppose I must not think of transmitting any separate account to England."

The beginning of 1770 could well mark the zenith of William Smith's career. He was the greatest intellectual power of the greatest city on the continent. The transit of Venus report was only one of a long series of astronomical accomplishments, which were no greater than his accomplishments in literature, education, and the church. He was included in every project thought of in Philadelphia, much as Franklin had been fifteen years earlier: when a "society for encouraging the culture of silk in Pennsylvania" was formed, it was automatic that he be one of its managers. He still had enemies, but none who doubted his ability: the worst of them—Franklin—was in England and might never return, and even Ezra Stiles had to admit, after an evening with him, that Smith was a "jolly priest." He could be charming when he chose to be, and in the early '70's he chose to be most of the time. Even in Charleston, where provincial council was then considering founding a South Carolina college, he was able to sweet-talk the citizenry out of £1000 for the College of Philadelphia in the winter of 1771.

Personally, he was also at the zenith of his life. He was forty-three years old, tall and solidly built, vigorous; and though his hair was starting to grey, he still had most of it. He had rafts of friends, most of whom owed him favors. He had six children, and two more to come, by a wife who adored him, and whom he adored. From Charleston, he wrote her, "Believe me, my ever dearest life, I am fully sensible my frequent absences have subjected you to many pains and solicitudes and inconveniences which, if God ever brings us together again, it shall be the business of my life to atone for by the continuance of every instance of tenderness that can contribute to your happiness."

But in the spring of 1770, irreparable things began to go wrong. The first blow came in April, when Rittenhouse, who had seemed so securely under Smith's thumb, sold his nearly completed orrery to the College of New Jersey at Princeton. "I never met with greater mortification," said Smith. "I thought I could depend, as much as on any thing under the sun, that after Mr. Rittenhouse knew my intentions about it, he would not have listened to any proposal for disposing of it . . . . to a village." President Witherspoon of Princeton had ridden over to Norristown and, after looking at the orrery, offered £300 for it, including some money down. Rittenhouse was perfectly able to accept, because he never had a cash deposit from Smith.

When news of the transaction was printed in the *Gazette,* Smith rushed out to Norristown. Rittenhouse had been "taken off his guard," Smith said; but the best satisfaction he could get was the promise that a second orrery should be offered the College—for a second

£300. Rittenhouse wrote Barton, "I would not, on any account, incur the imputation of cunning; nor are there, probably, many persons living who deserve it less: yet I am greatly mistaken if this matter does not, in the end, turn out to my advantage."

It did not turn out to Smith's advantage. To him, getting the first orrery was an "honor" which had now escaped him, his institution, and his province; and there may be some truth to his claim, "I had constantly told him, that if Assembly did not take it, I would take it for our College, and would have paid the full sum, should I have begged the money." Less likely is his claim that Rittenhouse himself was chagrined over selling to Witherspoon. Rittenhouse acted deliberately, and with great cunning; and he did it because he doubted that Smith would ever really pay him for the orrery, however much he might mean to. After all, he had never paid for the one-handed clock.

In August, 1770, the two-year-old Phineas Smith died. He was the first child his parents lost, which was remarkable, for an eighteenth century family of six; but his death cannot have been the easier for that. Fortunately, the Smiths had religion to help them; for the Church of England, though weak in theology, cleaves to the afterlife as the one belief that makes any sense of Christianity. The Anglican afterlife has no compartments: no limbo for those who have not been muttered over in certain ways, no hell for those who have more grievously failed the ritual. We are all to be with God, for we have all repented, have we not? Who is to say, in the last instant of any man's consciousness, that he has not repented? And what more is needed, beyond that private instant? Nothing but ceremony to comfort the survivors: a ceremony so rich, so brief, so immediately credible that the bitterest mourner is borne up, and no skeptics leave the door that many entered, though no one can say exactly what it is that he does believe.

When not about burying the dead, however, the Church of England can be as contentious as any. William Smith became missionary to Trinity Church, Oxford, nine miles northeast of Philadelphia, in 1766. The church had about one hundred and fifty members, though most of them had not been baptized and could not receive communion, because Infant baptism seemed wrong to them, and adult baptism seemed embarrassing.

Smith was made very welcome—his predecessor having defected to a richer parish in Maryland—and in the beginning thought of himself as a temporary preacher there. For a permanent preacher the parishioners favored Thomas Barton, who didn't want the job, and not old Sturgeon, who very much did. Meanwhile, Smith rode out to preach once every couple of weeks, and "suffered them to vote and enter me in their books as their minister till September next or longer if it suits me." He took less money for his services than he could have gotten, and when he had been there two years, he was still saying that he would be "glad to be released from the fatigue."

By 1771, however, he felt differently about it. "It is at present a pleasure to me, independent of some benefit it is to my large family," he wrote to the secretary of the Society for the Propagation of the Gospel. A new roof had been put on the building, and Smith was now taking all the money he was entitled to. He said he had the congregation pretty well in order, having expelled "one or two quarrelsome people." The rest were "more desirous than ever" to have him continue.

Actually, the congregation was at sixes and sevens

over him, and some would have settled for Sturgeon or anyone else, just to be rid of him. Though he did preach "occasionally," as one of them wrote to the secretary, many disliked him so much that they would not attend. As for the other duties of a preacher, Smith simply was not there to make pastoral calls or bury the dead. The congregation wanted a preacher who "by his good example, purity of manners, sound doctrine, and good advice gradually conduct them to happiness. . . . Pray send them an affable, kind and courteous English clergyman." But the Society had none to send, and the curt Scot continued their preacher until the Revolution.

Some of the time Smith saved by not preaching regularly at Oxford he devoted to a new interest: canals. He was enthusiastic about them because they would bring riches to Philadelphia, and because they would increase the value of his own hinterland properties, most of which lay along unimproved watercourses. Even when he started buying in Huntingdon and Bedford, he may have realized that the Juniata Valley was the one possible water route between Philadelphia and the Ohio country. Though he was a ferry proprietor at the Falls, and though ferrymen were constantly fighting with river navigators who cut their ropes, he realized that there was more to be made in opening up the back country than in operating a ferry. Besides, the ferry was leased out.

Assembly, which had been spending some money since 1761 to make the bed of the Schuylkill more navigable, now projected a canal to join the Schuylkill with the Susquehanna. In 1770, it appointed Smith and John Lukens to a committee which "leveled and examined" the high ground between the Tulpehocken

Creek, which is the westernmost tributary of the Schuylkill, and the Swatara Creek, which is the easternmost tributary of the Susquehanna. They thought it feasible to build the canal because, from ground higher than the pass, adequate water could be brought down to feed the locks. They even made an estimate of the cost of construction; and three years later Rittenhouse made a more elaborate survey and arrived at a somewhat higher cost, though it still within reason. Rittenhouse was appointed one of the commissioners for implementing the survey, but the project languished in spite of Smith's enthusiasm because many people—and particularly Rittenhouse—were being sucked out of daily life and into Revolutionary politics.

Smith continued to be interested in daily subjects. It would be wonderful to know more about his surveying trips, or any of the hundreds of trips he took into the back country. Did he let his beard grow? Did he carry his whiskey with him, or did he drink whatever he came across on route? On the nights when they had to camp out, what did he and Lukens say to each other across the fire? But because he was a practical man, he wrote down only what he saw and reasoned, not what he felt. Feeling was for poetry and letters home. He made no record of the personal details of his trips, and we must imagine them as best we can.

# 6 ❧ The Revolution

In February, 1771, William Smith began a series of twenty-three public lectures at the College to raise money for the orrery. At the introductory lecture, said Richard Peters, a crowded hall "swallowed every word he said, with the pleasure that attends eating the choicest viands." Later lectures in the series were given by Dr. Rush and by Rittenhouse himself, using the Princeton orrery for demonstration. According to Peters, Smith raised enough money to pay for the Philadelphia orrery, but twenty years later Rittenhouse said that he had never received more than an initial £109/10 on account from Smith—though he had, of course, received £300 from Assembly as a testimonial. What happened to the rest of the orrery money—whether, in fact, more than £109 ever was collected—it is now impossible to say. At the time, Rittenhouse's business acumen was obscured by the death of his first wife.

"The loss of his wife has greatly disconcerted him; but we try to keep up his spirits under it," wrote Smith, who never stopped liking and admiring Rittenhouse, though he skinned him when he could, and it was obvious that Rittenhouse did not like *him*. The next year they worked together to advance Pennsylvania's interest in the boundary dispute with Virginia, which was resulting in overlapping land claims in the western part of the province, especially around Pittsburgh. John Lukens went west and observed the appearances and disappearances of Jupiter's satellites, at the same time that Smith and Rittenhouse were observing them in Philadelphia. Their evidence showed Pittsburgh to be six miles inside Pennsylvania (the modern settlement puts it twenty-seven miles inside) by the terms of Penn's charter, which allowed the province five degrees of longitude; but it was also within Virginia's charter, if "west and northwest" were literally interpreted; and the issue was not settled until after the Revolution.

In 1772, Smith published the poems of Nathaniel Evans, who had been dead five years. In his introduction, he allowed that he had made "some corrections" to the poems, because "but few of them were revised by himself, with a view to being published." Evans by Smith is sometimes better than Evans by Evans, as when he changes "Long have we, lost in grateful wonder, viewed. . . ." to "In grateful wonder lost, long have we viewed. . . ." However, from Evans's forty-eight line poem to Franklin and his armonica, Smith deleted the sixteen most complimentary lines.

At the time there were few Philadelphians to dispute Smith's interpretation of Evans, or of most else. In spite of some reversals, he was still an enormously successful man. He had been, for several years, a secretary of the American Philosophical Society, and was elected president of the St. Andrew's Society in 1772. He was, off and on, the Grand Secretary of the Freemasons.

When schools or churches were to be founded, when great men died and needed a funeral sermon, when any occasion needed the stamp of dignity and authority, people turned to the brilliant—if slovenly and not always predictable—Dr. Smith.

Smith was meanwhile busy with additions to his house at the Falls. He also built a new boathouse and wharf for his ferry. In 1773, he sold to John—nephew of Thomas—Penn one hundred and forty-one acres on the west bank of the Schuylkill, for £10 an acre. He didn't take an especially high profit, because he had paid £6 or £7 for it ten years before; but he owed the Penns a great deal, and didn't mind repaying a little of it to John, who was almost his contemporary and was then lieutenant-governor of the province.

Perhaps with the idea of recouping his loss, or his lost profit, he wrote the trustees of the College, explaining, "When you consider the advanced price of necessaries, and the growing expense of a growing family. . . . I cannot make the sum of three hundred and fifty pounds a year, which I receive from you, answer my annual expenses, house-rent, &." He suggested that, if the College wanted its provost to maintain a proper dignity, it should build him a house on the grounds, which would put him "at least nearly on an equal footing with gentlemen in like station." The trustees unanimously agreed, and a 40 x 34 three-storey house was completed at the corner of Fourth and Arch Streets in 1776.

To protect his investments in western Pennsylvania, Smith wrote in 1774 *An Examination of the Connecticut Claim to Lands in Pennsylvania.* By one of its early charters, Connecticut could claim lands westward of New York that lay within its own latitude; and

in 1753 a Connecticut-based land company had bought
from the Six Nations a large tract—including the Wyoming Valley—in northeastern Pennsylvania. Not until
fifteen years later did the Six Nations, who still understood sale to mean right to use, but not exclusive right,
sell the same tract to the Penns.

Connecticut men and women began settling in the
Wyoming Valley. They were driven off once by Indians, and a second time by a force of Pennsylvanians
sent north for the purpose by John Penn. In the next
few years, a series of acrimonious but relatively blood-
less battles was fought between Yankees and Pennsylvanians, who alternately besieged each other in a log
fort the Yankees had built. By 1774, it had been in
Yankee hands for several years. Connecticut land titles
were honored, and Pennsylvania titles were worthless.

Smith held Pennsylvania title to undeveloped
tracts in the Wyoming Valley, and he also owned several thousand improved acres farther down the Susquehanna, near Sunbury in Northumberland county,
which were included in Connecticut's claim and which
Connecticut might eventually seize, if it was able to
maintain its claim to the east. Without mentioning
these in his book, he took up the legality of Connecticut's "wild chimera of a visionary brain." He reviewed
the history of Connecticut's borders, and asked whether
"lands westward as far as the South Sea" must be left
uninhabited "through many generations, for claims of
settlements to be made by the unborn progeny of Connecticut." He assured his fellow Pennsylvanians, "It
would be culpable to give way," and that a delayed settlement might have to be "written in blood."

Ezra Stiles, who kept a diary as if all history depended upon it, wrote in February, 1776, "On the 21st
of Dec. last a battle happened at Susquehanna between

200 Connecticut men and 6 or 700 (perhaps 200) Pennsylvanians, in which several were killed. A land contest. A ministerial stratagem to excite confusion, set on foot and promoted chiefly by Dr. Smith, the ambitious Tory provost of Philadelphia College." The Yankees won the battle, and held the Wyoming Valley until 1782, when Connecticut relinquished her very questionable claim to land that was, beyond question, included in the charter of Pennsylvania. By that time, Smith was in Chestertown, Maryland, working for a new college; and Stiles, who was made president of Yale in 1778, was finding new sticks to beat him with.

Ezra Stiles's long friendship with Benjamin Franklin does not entirely explain his hatred of William Smith. Though he and Smith were both preachers who became college presidents, they were opposites in everything. Stiles was a dissenter, so naive and ungraceful as to sign his letters "your affectionate brother in the gospel." He feared the Church of England, "an asylum for polite vice and irreligion." In his diary, he made lists of college presidents he had known and not known, and kept count of the thousand or more parish calls he made when he was a preacher, so that he could compare this year's figure to last year's. When he calls Smith a "consumate hypocrite in religion and politics," he means that Smith is playing a sophisticated game whose rules he doesn't understand and from which he feels himself to be excluded. He notes Smith's salary, and he envies him his social connections and his chic. "I know him personally, though I am not a witness to his immoralities," he says. Had he witnessed them, he wouldn't even have recognized them: he would have been a child observing—with bitterness and confusion —the vices of a man.

The naiveté of Stiles made him a revolutionary

from a very early time. Smith, on the other hand, was always in favor of Americans asserting their rights, but always opposed to absolute separation from England. His attitude was a radical one in 1765, when he wrote to the Dean of Gloucester to oppose the Stamp Act; it became a respectable one in 1774 and a reactionary one in 1776. Nonetheless, Smith had such good reasons for his attitude that he maintained it until it nearly ruined him.

Smith opposed independence because he saw an uncertain future for the Church of England in an independent America, and hence an uncertain future for himself. When the first Continental Congress met, Smith was forty-seven, an ideal age to be slipping into that pair of Episcopal sleeves that Benjamin Rush told John Adams he was admiring. The initial American bishops would have to be consecrated in England, for the English king was just as firmly a spiritual as a temporal ruler, examples like James II notwithstanding. Though the movement for an American bishopric had been successfully opposed for many years—by dissenters and politicians on both sides of the Atlantic, and by many important churchmen in England—the movement was still strong; and as late as 1776 Smith told Francis Alison that the American Anglicans were "determined" to have bishops.

Being cut off from England would also cut Smith off from his patrons, the Penns. Though John and his cousin Richard Penn had been in Philadelphia for some years, the aging Thomas retained the family's political and financial muscle; and when he died in 1775, his wife seems to have inherited much of it. Smith, who had improved his own position in the world in the twenty years since he had first met

Thomas Penn, did not need handouts as he once had;
but his friendship with the family was still one basis of
his power. And Great Britain was his native country: in
moving to America and becoming an American, he had
not had to stop thinking of himself as an Englishman
and a Scot also. He remembered that he had once been
unjustly imprisoned by Americans, and reprieved only
by the cool judiciousness of Englishmen. British laws
and the British constitution were a safeguard: he feared
that, should Americans win absolute power over their
land, they would prove to be bigoted, arbitrary, venge-
ful, and even murderous. In Pennsylvania, he proved to
be remarkably correct.

The events of 1774 and even of 1775 did not at the
time look as if they must inevitably lead to revolution
and independence. They looked more like a good, self-
righteous scrap, and Smith was all for that. He was a
member of Philadelphia's Committee of Correspondence, and when Paul Revere arrived with a letter from
the people of Boston, asking what should be done
about the closing of their port, Smith wrote the committee's reply. "If satisfying the East India Company for
the damage they have sustained would put an end to
this unhappy controversy and leave us on the footing of
constitutional liberty for the future, it is presumed that
neither you nor we could continue for a moment in
doubt what part to act; for it is not the value of the tax,
*but the indefeasible right of giving and granting our
own money* (A RIGHT FROM WHICH WE CAN
NEVER RECEDE), that is now the matter in consideration." The letter recommended a *"general congress* of
deputies from the different colonies" (an idea others
had had for some time) and trade restrictions only as a
last resort.

The first Continental Congress met in Philadelphia in September, 1774. The Pennsylvania delegation included Thomas Mifflin, a graduate of the College and Smith's neighbor at the Falls, but not Smith himself. In spite of his vocation, he would have been glad to serve, if chosen; but Assembly did the choosing. He got a chance to meet the delegates from the other colonies, and the delegates met him. "Septr. 1. Thursday. This day we breakfasted at Mr. Mifflin's," John Adams wrote. "Mr. C. Thomson came in, and soon after Dr. Smith. The famous Dr. Smith, the Provost of the College. He appears a plain man—tall, and rather awkward—there is an appearance of art." Silas Deane wrote, "Tomorrow, am invited by Dr. Smith, who is vastly sociable (or rather aims at it) to see the College and the curiosities of the city. . . ."

Congress did pass trade restrictions before adjourning. When the second Continental Congress met, in May, 1775, it was not in as faithful and prayerful a mood as the first had been. It knew what had happened three weeks earlier at Lexington and Concord, and it had had time to digest George III's dictum, "The dye is now cast, the colonies must either submit or triumph." Its resolution was further stiffened by Benjamin Franklin, just home from fruitless and humiliating negotiations in London. When Congress took part of the day off, on May 17, to attend the commencement of the College, it expected more than an academic exercise.

Part of the program Smith prepared was intended to honor Thomas Penn, whose death notice had just been received. There were also prayers by Smith and Alison, and Smith's customary charge to the graduates; but the political core of the ceremony was an oration,

"The Fall of Empires," delivered by William Moore Smith, William Smith's oldest child and a member of the graduating class. The falling empire in question was not the British but the American one; and empires fell, the fifteen-year-old orator warned, because they grew fat on imported luxuries. Thus a reason—other than the political one—was found for the non-importation resolutions of the first Congress; and the delegates to the second Congress must have left commencement shaking their heads at their own intuition.

In June, Smith was asked to preach to the militia of Philadelphia, assembled in Christ Church. For a text, he chose Joshua XXII:22; "The Lord God of Gods—the Lord God of Gods—He knoweth and Israel He shall know—if it be in rebellion or in transgression against the Lord—save us not this day!" Like so much of the Bible, this passage at first appears merely crude, repetitious, and inane; but Smith explained it by saying that it was written at a white heat, when nine and a half tribes of Israel, living on one side of the Jordan, were preparing to shellac the remaining two and a half tribes, living on the other side, over the erection of a separate altar. Luckily, an embassy from the nine and a half crossed the river and learned that the new altar was not intended as a competitor, and was not dedicated to a different god. Fratricide was averted.

Smith said he hoped he would be heard by every Englishman, especially those who "have meditated war and destruction against their brother-tribes in this our American Gilead. . . . Like the tribes of Reuben and Gad, we have chosen our inheritance, in a land separated from our fathers and brethren, not indeed by a small river, but an immense ocean. This inheritance we likewise hold by a plain original contract, entitling us to all the natural and improvable advantages of our situation, and to a community of priveleges with our brethren, in every civil and religious respect; except in this, that the throne or seat of Empire, that great altar at which the men of this world bow, was to remain among them. . . . But what high altars have we built to alarm our British Israel? . . . No embassy of great or good men has been raised, to stay the sword of destruction, to examine into the truth of our case, and save the effusion of kindred blood. . . .

"But I will weary you no longer with fruitless lamentations concerning those things that might be done. The question now is—since they are not done, must we tamely surrender any part of our birthright, or of that great charter of priveleges, which we not only claim by inheritance, but by the express terms of our colonization? I say, God forbid! For here, in particular, I wish to speak so plain that neither my own principles, nor those of the church to which I belong, may be misunderstood."

He praises liberty, freedom, constitutional rights, and even the "Genius of America"; but he nowhere uses the word *independence*. "To draw the line, and say where submission ends and resistance begins, is not the province of ministers of Christ." He closes by urging support for the law, and for civil liberties. "In a contest for liberty, think what a crime it would be, to suffer one freeman to be insulted, or wantonly injured in his liberty, so far as by your means it may be prevented."

The sermon was enthusiastically received by the militia, was printed by them, and went through at least thirteen editions in the next year. "It exceeds in style and sentiment anything I ever heard on the subject," said Silas Deane; and even Franklin sent copies of it to London. Smith sent one to the Bishop of London, and covered it with a long letter, signed by all the Anglican preachers in Philadelphia, saying, "The time is now come, My Lord," etc. Covering the cover letter was Smith's own letter, saying that all this insubordinate talk was really to England's advantage, if she would only see it. He might also have added that it was to the advantage of the Church of England. He was beginning to see, as he wrote to the secretary of the Society for the Propagation of the Gospel two days later, that if the church did not side with the colonists soon, "we should not have the appearance of a church or people left." In that extremity, he was reconciled to war; but he was not reconciled to—he could not imagine—independence.

Meanwhile, other Pennsylvanians were rapidly growing more bumptious. Proprietary government became impossible to enforce, and Richard Penn went back to England in the summer of 1775, carrying copies of Smith's sermon and the letters to the Bishop. The governor's Provincial Council met for the last time in October, and the province—or colony or commonwealth or whatever it was—was governed by an increasingly radical Assembly, and by various quasi-legal committees, such as the Council of Safety. Perhaps the most obnoxious was a Committee of Observation and Inspection, whose business it was to investigate un-Americanism. In January, 1776, they examined the conduct of "Parson Smith," for having "spoken and acted very disrespectfully of Congress and all our proceedings." They had a witness primed, but the man's conscience must have bothered him: he spoke so ambiguously that the committee was enraged with him, but concluded "that no hold could, at present, be taken of Smith." Nevertheless, they kept an eye on him, and in March they were glad to be informed that he had said to some friends "that Great Britain would mortgage America for as much money as would enable her to conquer it." They were keeping a file on Parson Smith, bless their little hearts.

Smith's political opinions were no secret: he wrote a series of eight letters, signed "Cato" after his usual custom but with no attempt made to conceal his identity, which appeared in the *Gazette* in March and April. In February, he delivered before Congress a funeral oration on General Richard Montgomery, who had fallen in an ill-advised attempt to storm Quebec on New Year's Eve, because his men's enlistments ran out on New Year's Day. Congress, Assembly, the city militia, even the Committee of Observation and Inspection joined in a processional through the streets, and Smith stepped out the door and joined them as they came past his house. It must have been one of the finest of the many processionals—political, educational, Masonic— that he loved to organize.

It led to the new German Calvinist Church, and was ushered in by an orchestra which Smith had assembled from Lancaster, York and Philadelphia. Smith opened the ceremony with a spate of quotations from classical poetry, all predicting glory in heaven for military heroes. Each phrase, as he spoke it, was echoed by the choir and accompanied by the orchestra. Smith was, as he said, "laying a wide foundation" for what he had to say about General Montgomery in particular.

The oration, which lasted over an hour, described Montgomery's career and praised the soldiers who had fallen with him before Quebec. However, it was understood that Smith *must* speak to the political situation, and when he did, he said that the general's loyalty to George III "remained firm and unshaken . . . . and could have been outweighed by nothing earthly, but the unquenchable love of liberty, and that sacred duty which we owe to ourselves and our posterity." He said he was sure everyone joined him in praying for a restoration of "the former harmony between Great Britain and these colonies."

He said too much. The passage about the restoration of harmony he took verbatim from Congress's most recent petition to the king; but the petition had been made in July, and it was now February. When Congress next met, a motion to thank Smith was made, but it was withdrawn when it became clear that the majority would not support it. The oration was "an insolent performance," said John Adams, and Smith's appointment to deliver it was "a great oversight and mistake." Smith published the text himself and defended it in a long footnote; but the majority was with Adams. "While we contend for liberty with others, let us not refuse liberty to each other," Smith had said two years before; but it was beginning to happen just the same.

The next time he spoke on politics, Smith took some care that it should be with anonymity. The pamphlet *Plain Truth,* an answer to Tom Paine's *Common Sense,* was almost certainly his work, though Thomas Jefferson wrote in the title page of his copy "by Alexander Hamilton." Like everything else Smith had written, *Plain Truth* defended the British Empire, though it also defended American rights. It gave him a good opportunity to take another cut at Benjamin Franklin by dwelling on his unpatriotic role in the Stamp Act controversy. When a mob descended on the house of another man whom it suspected of being the author, Smith must have been very glad he had not signed his name to the pamphlet.

If Smith was beginning to suffer from the abridgement of liberty that accompanied American independence, some of his old enemies were faring even worse. Isaac Hunt, who had written "Exercises in Scurrility Hall" ten years before, now wrote pamphlets in defense of England until a mob stormed his house, put him in a cart, paraded him through the streets, and gave him "a narrow escape from tarring and feathering," according to his son, Leigh. William Franklin, an equally determined loyalist, was arrested by the New Jersey militia for continuing to act as Royal Governor. "Mrs. Franklin and I have been most abominably abused by a most abominable mob," he wrote. He was incarcerated in Connecticut for several years, while his wife died slowly and pitifully in New Jersey.

As recommended by Congress, a Pennsylvania constitutional convention met in July, 1776. Presided over by Benjamin Franklin, it wrote the most radical and at the same time oppressive document of the Revolution: it began with a bill of rights, and went on to establish a unicameral legislature, an executive council, and a council of censors. It was "ordained" by the convention, and was never submitted to the people for ratification. A new Assembly had hardly met under it before a law was passed requiring every man to take a test oath of allegiance, including a promise to peach on "all treasons or traitorous conspiracies." William Smith, who was trying to keep the College intact and didn't need any more trouble from government, took the oath immediately; but many Pennsylvanians objected, including Thomas Smith, who was a colonel of the militia, a justice of the peace in Bedford County, and a sometime Assemblyman. He refused to release to Assembly the records of who had taken the oath in Bedford until they imprisoned him for it.

After the Declaration of Independence, Smith made no further effort to thwart separation from England. He withdrew from politics and concentrated on saving his personal fortune and on guarding his College. Three months after the Declaration, and perhaps with a view to protecting the College from the rapidly depreciating continental currency, he bought for it about six hundred acres, including the entire site of Norristown and Barbadoes Island in the Schuylkill, for £6000. And in November, he observed another transit of Mercury from the College grounds. He wrote, "This year exhibiting little else but scenes of confusion and distress amidst the calamities of an unhappy war, scarce any attention was paid, by members of the American Philosophical Society, to astronomical or any other literary subjects." Nevertheless, he set up the telescopes, and sent to hasten Lukens and Rittenhouse (the latter, a member of the Council of Safety, may well have been promulgating regulations unto the commonwealth). They came and looked, and afterward Smith made the calculations and wrote up the report for the American Philosophical Society, which never published it. In January, 1777, he got Rittenhouse over to observe a partial eclipse of the sun. It was so cold that the clock stopped running.

The College survived the first years of the war. In the fall of 1775, Benjamin Franklin allowed his grandson, the second of three generations of sinister sons to grace the Franklin family, to enter the Latin school. It was quite a concession for Benjamin, who had once said he would never give Smith another meeting; but Franklin was nearly seventy now, and so busy arguing for independence as to put aside old grudges for the time being. William Temple Franklin was fifteen years old and full of beans: two hours a day, Dr. Smith taught him mathematics, "of which I begin to understand something"; but he didn't think he could enjoy dancing lessons "when the thoughts of making a Latin theme is sticking in my stomach." It was his first trip to America: he had been raised by his grandfather since his father married and assumed the governorship of New Jersey. When Benjamin left to become minister to France, William Temple went with him as his secretary, and never returned to the College.

Though Smith's second son, Thomas Duncan, graduated from the College in 1776, commencement was more somber than it had been the year before, and Congress did not attend. Washington had forced Howe to evacuate Boston in March; but Howe was in Halifax strengthening his army, and he might soon sail for New York or the Chesapeake or even Philadelphia. The Declaration of Independence impended.

There was no commencement at all in 1777. Troops had been billeted on the College for a couple of years, off and on; but in January, 1777, the faculty finally appealed to the Council of Safety: "Before we could well clear away the dirt and filth left by one set of soldiers, and meet again in our places, another set has been forced upon us; owing to which, we have scarce yet been able to collect together a third part of the former number of our youth." They reminded the council that, as an educational institution, they were entitled to protection "in all civilized states," and asserted that if

*One-handed clock built by*
*David Rittenhouse for William Smith*

*Political cartoon of 1765.*
*Smith is probably the leftmost clerical figure*

*Washington College Architect's elevation*

*Falls of Schuylkill in 1794, with "Smith's Octagon" at top left*

quartering continued the College must either move or break up. In desperation, they begged only that they be *notified* before they became the involuntary hosts of the military.

In July, the trustees formally closed the College. General Howe, who had held New York for nearly a year, was expected to march on the capital that summer; and Washington waited for him in central Jersey, without any real hope of stopping him. The College and Academy students had gone home with no expectation of returning in the fall; so closing the institutions meant little more than stopping the faculty salaries, which must have hurt some much more than it did Smith.

Nonetheless, it was an exasperating summer for him, with soldiers everywhere he looked. He and his wife and seven children—including two college graduates and a year-old baby—had to stay in town because the house at the Falls of Schuylkill was taken over by General Stephens of the Virginia militia. A board of general officers, presided over by the fast-moving George Washington, sat there on August 7, trying to straighten out the army's financial muddles. Shortly afterward Smith, unusually boisterous and undoubtedly drunk, got mad enough at the depredations to his property to slug a captain of the New Jersey militia. The captain slugged him back, and though Smith hollered and tried to get the captain court martialed, Washington and the court dismissed the charge, saying that he "deserved the treatment he received."

The end of August, when news came that Howe had landed his army at Elkton, Maryland, and was advancing on Philadelphia from that direction, Washington marched south to forestall him; but Philadelphians prepared to abandon the city, as they had done on a false rumor the summer before. The Supreme Executive Council then sent a militia officer to examine Smith's private papers and—when that turned up no evidence of treason—it issued warrants for the arrest of Smith and forty other persons who, it thought, might have "evinced a disposition inimical to the cause of America" (i.e., to itself). Smith was paroled when he swore not to express himself politically and to appear whenever summoned; but seventeen Quakers, who would not swear, were carted off to Winchester, Virginia, and kept there many months, though no charge was ever made against them.

The charges against Smith were never stated either, but they were mostly for keeping bad company. Thomas Barton, Rittenhouse's brother-in-law and a close associate of Smith's in the Society for the Propagation of the Gospel, was an overt Loyalist, as were many other Anglican preachers, though less so in Pennsylvania than in Maryland and New York. Old William Moore, Smith's father-in-law, was such a Loyalist that when patriot troops came to search Moore Hall for arms, he broke his sword in half rather than give it to them. Richard Peters died six days after the Declaration of Independence and most of the other supporters of the proprietors, like the old Chief Justice William Allen, were Loyalists too, though none of them was militant or military enough to do much about it. Smith had been close to all of them.

On September 9, Washington failed to stop Howe at Brandywine Creek, twenty-five miles southwest of the city. Congress and Assembly fled to Lancaster, and most patriots who had something to lose fled with them. Howe feinted, outmaneuvered Washington, and marched into Philadelphia almost without firing a shot on September 26. Washington attacked him at Germantown October 5, but was beaten off, and withdrew to build his winter camp at Valley Forge.

Smith did not go to Lancaster. He split up his family, sending his oldest son, William Moore, to Moore Hall to be with his grandfather, and his oldest daughter, Williamina, to the house of her aunt, Mrs. Phineas Bond, in Philadelphia. With the rest of the family he moved to a house on the College's newly acquired Barbadoes Island, which was just within the American lines but which, from its isolation, might be left alone by both belligerents. From there he sent a doggerel answer to Major Bruen, an American officer in charge of foraging, who demanded to know the number and condition of his horses:

> Accept these lines good Master Bruen
> Unless you mean to be my ruin—
>
> My list of HORSES and their gear
> You ask. The first a sorrel *Mare*.
> Her age, last summer, was twice seven,
> And sorely crippled with the SPAVIN,
> But thin of flesh & little marrow,
> Was never yoked to plow or harrow,
> Nor yet to chaise or cart or wagon,
> And her weak back ne'er bore a bag on;
> With her my daughter learned to ride,
> And *prays* to keep her—'til a bride.
> A FILLY three years old last summer,
> Not broke—too slim even for a drummer;
> Claimed by my son, now full eighteen,
> Who hopes to mount her—next campaign.
> Dear spouse and I with HORSES two,
> To church or fair were wont to go;

The men with WHISKERS took the best,
Worth thirty *sterling pounds* confessed;
The other scarce will drag us thro'
The miry roads & winter's snow.
Of all my stock, two *horses* more
Only remain, their age two score,
Hackneyed and slow, my fields to till,
Or with crazed team, and fractured wheel,
To drag some sticks thro' paths uneven
To warm a wife & children seven—
My winter's beef and mutton gone,
My fields laid waste, my fences flown,
The damage spread throughout my grounds,
Exceeding twice three hundred pounds.

    Of all these facts pray take inspection
    And for what's left grant me *protection*.

The gist of Smith's poem, of course, is that he cannot possibly spare any of his five horses. In spite of that, a troop of soldiers drove off his cattle and his favorite horse later in the fall. He appealed to Washington, who returned him the cattle, but paid him for the horse in continental currency.

As a preacher, Smith enjoyed a good deal of freedom to go back and forth between the lines, visiting relatives and attending to the buildings of the College. In November, when the British had made themselves secure in Philadelphia, they laid siege to an earthenwork fort below the city which was still held by the patriots and which, by commanding the *chevaux de frise* in the channel, were keeping the Delaware closed to British supply ships. Smith took a large telescope and went down to the mouth of the Schuylkill, the better to watch the fun. He had a number of friends with him, and it must have been quite a picnic. Later, he was accused of saying, "If they don't surrender, they ought every man of them to be put to the sword." He denied it, but it does sound like his habit of thought, if not his manner of speech. At any rate he was right: the British had worked a cutdown Indiaman into a creek behind the fort, so that she was able to bombard the defenders with impunity; and after a good many rounds from her, the garrison did surrender.

Smith did not stop traveling, just because Philadelphia was in British hands. He probably saw Bedford, if not Huntingdon, that winter, for he was working on a large and complicated land deal with George Croghan. In March, he went up to the Wyoming Valley to attend a meeting of the Pennsylvania land claimants; but nothing came of it because the Six Nations, who had joined with the English the year before, swooped down on the valley in July, massacring many settlers and driving off the others. The whole upper Susquehanna was Indian territory again.

Of greatest concern to Smith in the winter of 1777–78 was the orrery of the College. Already, the Princeton orrery had lost most of its moving parts to wounded patriots who were nursed back to health in Nassau Hall and took the funny little gears home as souvenirs. Smith went to General Howe and asked permission to lock the orrery room up from the rest of the College, which was being used as a British military hospital. He made himself a kind of steward over the orrery, kept the keys with him, and showed it only when he was present to protect it, so that no damage came to it during the entire occupation.

Philadelphia was never gayer than it was that winter: while offal filled the streets and every kind of municipal service broke down, Loyalists threw open their doors to the British and, to a lesser extent, to the Hessians. Assembly, cramped in Lancaster, grew testy and lashed out as best it could with an "Act for Suspending the Powers of the Trustees of the College and Academy of Philadelphia for a Limited Time." The limited time was to begin retroactively on September 1, 1777, and was to last until three months after the British evacuation, whenever that might be. Meanwhile, the trustees were to retain enough power to pay full salaries to Alison and all the other faculty who had fled, but nothing to those who had "voluntarily put themselves under subjection to the enemy." The fleeing faculty, in other words, were to be paid by the *College* for what prestige they might add to the *government*.

In peacetime, there is precious little place for a man who wishes to go about his own business; and in wartime there is none at all. Caring whether a college survives is thought mean, when tea drinkers must pay a small tax on their habit. Caring about one's own family is thought selfish, when one can shoulder a gun and shoot someone else's. The practical man is eschewed, and is assumed to be an enemy, and thus it is not surprising that at the time when the patriot Committee on Observation and Inspection was trying to incarcerate Smith, a Loyalist preacher in New York was denouncing him for "rushing headlong into rebellion."

Throughout the Revolution, William Smith kept up his correspondence with Thomas Penn's widow in England. He preached whenever a congregation could be assembled, and no doubt he baptized children and buried the dead, too. There is no record of his having visited Washington's camp, and it is certain that he took no part in the gay life of Philadelphia. He was furious when he learned that Mrs. Bond had let his daughter Willy play a lady to one of the Knights of the Burning Mountain in the *Meschianza.*

The *Meschianza* was a ball given by the British officers in honor of General Howe, who was being replaced by General Clinton. As staged by Captain—later Major—John André, the seven hundred and fifty guests, all in their prescribed costumes, were rowed down the Delaware from Kensington to Southwark, promenaded between troops and through triumphal arches, and entertained with a mock joust, fireworks, dancing, Pharoah, and a dinner served by black slaves in Oriental dress. André was Willy's suitor, and he had du Simitiere paint two portraits of his sixteen-year-old sweetheart: the first a watercolor, showing her in her *Meschianza* costume, "a high turban and veil ornamented with black feather jewels, gold lace, and spangles," and a white silk harem outfit also ornamented with gold. She posed in the attitude in which she received from her knight the trophies of the mock joust. Though born on the Fourth of July, Willy was no Yankee Doodle Dandy.

The second portrait was an oval miniature, oil on porcelain, one half by three quarters of an inch, set in a ring. It showed a beautiful but arch young woman, wearing a bonnet and a rat in her hair. André gave Willy the miniature but kept the watercolor for himself, perhaps because of its association with trophies.

In a way, the *Meschianza* was a farewell by the British officers to Philadelphia, as well as to Howe. As soon as Clinton became commander, he held a council of war and decided to evacuate the city. On June 18, the main body of the army withdrew, followed so closely by Washington's scouting parties that several laggard officers were captured; and within a week the state and federal governments moved back into town.

William Smith had hardly moved his family back to the provost's house when, on June 24, he was setting up his telescope again in the College yard. Rittenhouse, Lukens, and Owen Biddle all came, but the morning was cloudy, and they did not see the sun until ten o'clock, when it appeared between clouds and showed them that the eclipse had already begun. The clouds dispersed at eleven, and they were able to note the moment when the eclipse ended. Smith wrote the report.

Other Philadelphians were more interested in political revenge than in astronomy. A few overt Loyalists who had meant to escape with the British were captured by the advancing patriot troops, and more were rounded up later. Anyone who had remained at home was suspect; but Smith applied for discharge from parole on June 30, and went around himself to get the papers the next afternoon. The streets were filthy, and many of the houses were a shambles, but Benedict Arnold—appointed by Washington to be military commander of the city—made Loyalist hunting the first order of business. In August, the first of a series of show trials was held, and ended with an execution on the common.

Spies, deserters, turncoats, and even those who had worked for the British in menial capacities were arrested, tried, and shot. In September, Abraham Carlisle, a carpenter, and John Roberts, a miller, were tried and sentenced to be hanged, the former for having been a gatekeeper at one of the British redoubts and the latter for having enlisted in the British army, though he had frequently used his uniform to curry mercy for patriots during the occupation. Both men were Quakers, and it was understood that their punishment was meant as an object lesson to other Quakers, most of whom had at least acquiesced to the British occupation.

William Smith, in spite of the precariousness of his own political reputation and his life-long quarrel with the Quakers, made himself a leader of the movement to have the sentences of Carlisle and Roberts commuted. A majority of the grand jurors and the petit jurors who had convicted them appealed for leniency, as did three hundred and eighty-seven petitioners, including Dr. Rush, General Cadwallader, and even the militia colonel who had examined Smith's papers the year before. But in November both men were hanged.

Loyalists who had left the city with the British and put themselves beyond reach of the noose lost everything they could not carry with them. Jacob Duché's house was taken for the residence of the state chief justice. The houses, mill, and German printing shop of the Christopher Sauers were confiscated and sold at low prices to patriotic citizens, with the purchase money going to the state. And of course the property of men like Carlisle and Roberts was not inherited by their children.

On September 25, with the expiration of Assembly's limited time suspension act, the trustees and faculty met to discuss the best way to get the College and Academy started again. Smith cannot have been too gregarious at the meeting: two-year-old Eliza, the baby of his family, died that day. Nonetheless, the various schools were reopened that fall, though most of the returning students were in the Academy, not the College. The April before, Assembly had passed a special act requiring "all trustees, provosts, rectors, professors. . . ." to take the despised test oath, and had included merchants, traders, and pharmacists for good measure; but

Smith had complied long before, and so had most of the faculty and trustees, so it seemed that all might yet go well, and there was even talk of granting degrees again.

After hours, Smith was giving some lectures in physics to army officers stationed in town. He seemed to be well on his way to reestablishing himself in Philadelphia: he was even asked to preach to the Masons on St. John's Day, December 28, 1778.

The Masonic processional went from the College to Christ Church, three blocks away. It was led by the sword bearer, followed by two wanded deacons, the three orders (architectural), the Bible and the Ahiman Rezon on red velvet cushions, a reverend brother, four wanded deacons, Brother William Smith and Brother George Washington, two pillared wardens, past and present masters, local officials, a band, visiting brethern, and "the members of the different lodges, walking two and two, according to seniority." Smith's sermon lavished praise on Washington. It seemed that all might go well.

In February, Assembly appointed a committee to examine the College and Academy. Right then, it was clear that all was not going to go well. Smith, who had been expecting a confrontation though hoping to avoid it, had already gotten some material together in defense of the institutions; and when Assembly's committee met with a committee of the trustees, he was able to present them with an elaborate history of the College, and a statement of its present condition. Assembly's committee listened attentively, and was not especially unfriendly; but Assembly itself, listening with a deaf ear, was going to make the final decision.

There were, at the time of Smith's report, forty

students in the Medical School, twenty-two in the College, eighty-one in the Academy, and fifty-seven in the Charity School, or a total enrollment of two hundred, compared to well over three hundred in most of the years before the Revolution. Finances were bad, because mortgages which the College owned were being paid off in depreciated currency. Paper money financed the Revolution, but it liquidated the endowment of the College of Philadelphia, for which Smith had spent two of the early years of his marriage away from home, wife, and family. In the same month that Assembly's committee heard the report, Smith and Alison complained to the trustees that *twice* their 1775 salaries, which they were now receiving, would not buy them subsistence in 1779, and both were given additional raises. For the sake of Assembly, the College's finances were made to seem sound in Smith's report; but actually they were not.

The committee reported to Assembly, but nothing was done before the summer recess. The College made fresh noises about granting degrees, but Supreme Executive Council President Joseph Reed, who had once been an Academy student himself but had transferred to Princeton shortly after Smith became provost, said that degree granting was inappropriate in wartime. In November, 1779, a newly elected Assembly passed an act "To confirm the estates and interests of the College, Academy, and Charitable School of the City of Philadelphia, and to amend and alter the charter thereof, conformably to the Revolution and to the constitution and government of this commonwealth, and to erect the same into an university." The next day, Francis Alison just died.

It was pretended that Assembly's act was only a

modification of the extant frame of the College, to bring it into conformity with the new political framework. In truth, the act dictated the demise of the College, and the usurpation of its buildings and funds by a wholly new institution, subservient to Assembly, and named the University of the State of Pennsylvania. It was exactly the same kind of swindle that cost the Loyalists their properties following the British evacuation; but the College being more formidable than any individual citizen, it took Assembly longer to nerve itself for the job. And although two of the old trustees had been Loyalists and were now living in England (Richard Penn and William Allen), there can be no doubt that the main object of Assembly's wrath was William Smith.

The act said, "It appears that seminaries of learning, when properly conducted, have been public blessings to mankind and that on the contrary, when in the hands of dangerous and disaffected men, they have troubled the peace of society, shaken the government, and often caused tumult, sedition, and bloodshed." It charged that the trustees had "departed from the plan of the original founders and had narrowed the foundation of the said institution" by a resolution passed in 1764, soon after Smith returned from his fund-raising trip to England. That resolution, designed to answer the charge that the College was becoming too Anglican, declared that the trustees would take care that the original charter "be not narrowed, nor the members of the Church of England or those dissenting from them . . . be put on any worse footing in this seminary than they were at the time of obtaining the royal brief." But if no sect could be put on a worse footing, no sect could aspire to a better, and therefore the charter was narrowed. It was a willful misinterpretation of the resolution, but it served the purpose.

On the other hand, Smith certainly had striven to advance his church, in the College and elsewhere. His letters to Thomas Penn had chortled with it, and he had loaded the board of trustees with Anglicans. He did it because he was naturally pugnacious, and because he understood that the Church of England, with its obscure and watery doctrines, was a good guarantee for everyone's liberties. It shot no one, it hanged no one, it confiscated no property. He never discriminated against dissenter students, though he was amused by their enthusiasms, and he was the only Anglican on the faculty for many years.

Assembly's act appointed a new board of twenty-five new trustees, including preachers of the largest sects, state officials (like Treasurer Rittenhouse and Admiralty Judge Hopkinson), and plain citizens to whom Assembly took a liking. An endowment was to be formed of confiscated estates, all new officers and faculty were to take yet another oath to the state, and all old officers and faculty were to hand over all books, records, real estate, and apparatus. Every one of the professors of the College was hired to teach in the University, except Smith. It was a monstrous stupidity: however bellicose and drunken Smith was, however dirty his academic robes, however foul his mouth, however often absent he was from his duties at the College, however venal, niggardly, spiteful, and mendacious, he was the greatest educator of eighteenth-century America; and in supplanting him Assembly doomed its new institution to mediocrity right away, and to failure at no very distant time.

Smith, for whom grace may have been a theologi-

cal concept or a proper name, but certainly not a manner, simply would not give up his College. A committee
of the new trustees—including Hopkinson, Ewing, and
the ever insensitive Rittenhouse—waited on him with
the demand that all property of the College be turned
over to them. He surrendered the papers and the use of
the buildings, but the symbols of power—the seal and
the keys—he kept, and he would not consider moving
out of the provost's house, which had been built for
him only three years before. Ewing, the new provost,
and Rittenhouse, the new vice-provost, hemmed and
hawed; but Smith was more determined than they
were, and they went away leaving him in possession.

It was a cold winter. In February, Smith and Rittenhouse hired a man to dig a hole on the common, so
that they could measure the depth of the frost (forty-
three inches). Smith, under civil if not military siege in
his own house, ruminated about what to do, perhaps
fondling the seal and keys as he did so. Francis Hopkinson, his former protégé, would soon be designing a new
seal, picturing the orrery, which now belonged to the
new University. Across the street from the provost's
house, classes were going on, and were being timed by
the one-handed clock. It was lucky he had never paid
for it. Smith took a drink and wrote some letters about
getting Washington made Grand Master of all Freemasons in the United States, but nothing came of it.

Smith was offered a parish in Chestertown, Kent
County, Maryland. Chestertown was a pleasant enough
place, but remote; and as the parish was not particularly rich, and was having some difficulty getting his
wages together, he appealed to Assembly his removal
from the College, and waited until the Chestertown vestry could assure him a payment of six hundred bushels

of wheat a year. At least he wouldn't starve, as he might well have on continental paper, which was losing forty percent of its vitamins each year.

Smith was in Chestertown by July, 1780, preaching a Fourth of July sermon to the country folk. He started teaching a few students in a private academy, but he didn't bring his family down until the fall, when he merged his academy with the Kent County Free School and became principal of the whole shebang. He then gave up the provost's house in Philadelphia, and just in time: the trustees of the University were sending constables around with eviction notices.

# 7 ❧ Chestertown

If William Smith learned anything from his dismissal
from the College of Philadelphia, he learned the folly
of his reliance on the house of Hanover. The house,
which had so far given England two brutish kings and a
demented one, had nonetheless held the loyalty of all
Anglican preachers because—whatever its dialect, whatever its manners, whatever its interests—it had supported the Church of England. In America, however, it
was now certain that the royal house could no longer
support Smith and his church, and that he must look
elsewhere.

Yet the habit of mind persisted: a preacher was
loyal to his church, of course, but did he not also look
up to temporal authority to assure both the continuity
of the church and the security of his own living? How
could a church which was a mass of theological contra-
dictions, which offered neither showy evangelism nor
magical transubstantiations, which had from its concep-
tion relied upon the temporal power—how could it
survive without political support? And if the church
could not survive, how could liberty, morality, and

property; how could individual preachers survive? If the king was dead, for all useful purposes, who could take his place in the loosely and perhaps only temporarily united States of America?

There was only one. Nominally, he was an Anglican, and he sometimes went to church, though he was never seen to take communion or to bow his head in prayer, and indeed such obeisance was offensive to his deistic convictions. He was far less intelligent than George III, but far more rational. He was a man of such character as no Hanover ever possessed, or ever aspired to. He had already received every honor the quarrelsome states could give, had fended off every rival with a firmness and diplomacy that only improved his reputation, had led the army and dragged the Congress through four years of triumphs, blunders, and antagonisms of which only he seemed to know the outcome. Should independence and unity survive in the states—and it seemed increasingly likely that they would—he would undoubtedly receive even greater honors, even higher offices. From the time of William Smith's removal to Chestertown, the "American Cincinnatus," as he had called him in his 1778 St. John's Day sermon, became for him everything that the Hanovers had been: the object of his adulation and prayers, the source of his hopes, the leader of his cause.

Unfortunately, George Washington did not like William Smith, and did not trust him either. Washington was willing to use Thomas Smith as a lawyer to evict squatters from his lands in western Pennsylvania, and he did dine at Thomas's at least once, and never at William's; but he valued Thomas the way we all value lawyers whom we retain to prosecute profitable but disreputable actions. Washington conducted an extensive

and courteous correspondence with Thomas; but
surely, had he lived until 1800 when Thomas at last
had a son and named him George Washington Smith,
he would have laughed up his sleeve.

For William Smith he had an aversion more pro-
nounced and more specific. He never saw him, save
when Smith engineered the occasion and forced him to
it. He never mentioned him, in his dry but voluminous
daybooks and directives, except in the dryest terms.
Even when the New Jersey militiaman was accused and
acquitted of slugging Smith, he is only mentioned as
"Dr. Smith." Dr. Smith! But he knew him well! The
closest Washington ever came to defending or praising
Smith was in a letter he wrote to a friend in 1790, when
Smith had been his flatterer and sycophant for ten or
twelve years: "Mr. Smith is a man of acknowledged
abilities, but it may not be well perhaps to say more in
a letter, especially as his reinstatement [as provost in
Philadelphia] may have given rise to a reform of that
conduct which did not escape censure formerly."

The nine years that Smith lived in Chestertown,
there was seldom a month when he did not visit Philadelphia. He was a commuter, as much as was possible
in the eighteenth century, when the hundred-mile trip
meant two days' travel, following a dirt track through
fields of wheat and tobacco, skirting or fording several
broad rivers, depending on the food and bedding and
whisky of crude brick inns along the way. Chestertown
was gorgeous: a river almost as wide as the Delaware,
and a cluster of one hundred houses, many of them
handsome, and many of them old enough to look at
home in the landscape. Chestertown offered him a position in the church, as well as in education; but he was
committed to Philadelphia. He was still a member of

the Philosophical Society, the St. Andrew's Society, the Masons. He still had his house at the Falls, kept open by his sister Isabella. He was still occasionally called to preach at the city's churches. His entire speculative capital was still invested in Pennsylvania lands; and he had no end of personal business to attend to in Philadelphia.

"It was difficult to know where he was to be found," James Madison wrote to Thomas Jefferson. Jefferson wanted a copy of a curious old map that Smith owned, which showed the South Sea to be only ten days' travel from the James River. When Madison finally got in touch with Smith, through Rittenhouse, Smith said he was "anxious to oblige," and would help make a copy himself, though he could not let the original out of his hands. Six months later, when Madison caught up with Smith in person, he learned that the copy was "not yet finished," but was promised that it would be soon. However, Smith never did send the copy to Jefferson, and Madison concluded, "He calculates the value of the chart on its being the single one remaining, and thinks the issuing of copies would depreciate it."

Smith was defending his property on every front: the College of Philadelphia had been illegally taken away from him, and it owed him money. He repeatedly appealed to the trustees of the new university, who were, as he tactfully told them, "robbing the original owners." His salary had been in arrears at the time of the "robbery," and he was owed money for the addition he had made to the provost's house (now occupied by Ewing), and for the annuity he had been voted on his return from the fund-raising trip to England in 1764.

In 1783, the trustees appointed a committee to ex-

amine Smith's financial claims, consisting of Rittenhouse, Francis Hopkinson, and William White. White
was a young Episcopal preacher, a graduate of the College of Philadelphia, and an admirer of Smith all his
life—though not an uncritical admirer. As part of their
examination, the committee went out to Norristown to
look over the farm the College owned, on which Smith
had lived during the British occupation, and for which
he was responsible. Finding that the pasture fences
were all standing and that Smith hadn't run off with
the doorknobs, the trustees followed the committee's
advice and allowed him part of the money he claimed
was owed him. It didn't shut him up.

Smith took his claim to the state legislature, lodg-
ing six appeals between 1780 and 1784. When the
Council of Censors met, he appealed to that. He
argued; he wrote letters; he defended his character to
all who would listen, and was quick to notice an enemy
or an ally. "I thank your Excellency," he wrote to Caesar Rodney, "for that gentlemanlike, liberal, and can-
did regard which I am well informed you have been
pleased to pay to my good name, when called in question by prejudiced and narrow-minded men." Life in
the great world was a battle, and he who had been part
of it for twenty-six years could not be happy in Chestertown. He concluded his letter to Rodney, "This little
quiet town produces no news."

He went up to Philadelphia to preach, or to attend
a meeting of the American Philosophical Society, or
even to see a play, such as the *Gustavus Vasa* that "my
college" put on. He proposed Washington for membership in the American Philosophical Society, an intellectual honor to which the general was not entitled, but
which, once it was proposed, no one could refuse him.

Smith, who was still a secretary of the society, wrote the letter notifying Washington of his election, and Washington had Alexander Hamilton answer for him, in polite but guarded language. After all, what could he do, refuse?

In the summer of 1780 Smith wrote, on behalf of the Pennsylvania Grand Lodge, to the Masonic lodges of the other states, proposing that a new office—Grand Master General of the Thirteen United American States—be created, and that Washington be elected to it. Massachusetts demurred, and the scheme was never carried out; but two years later, when Smith's abridgement and revision of the *Ahiman Rezon* was published by the Pennsylvania Grand Lodge, it was dedicated to Washington by "his Excellency's most humble servant, and faithful Brother, William Smith, Grand Secretary." Washington is not known to have acknowledged this compliment at all.

But Smith did not spend all his time in Philadelphia pushing his own interests. As he himself had straddled the Revolution, some of his friends had fallen to one side and some to the other, and he now did what he could for those who were more compromised than he was. Most conspicuous and most pitiful was Elizabeth Graeme Fergusson.

Elizabeth Graeme, the daughter of a rich and sociable doctor, was ten years younger than William Smith. At seventeen, she was pretty, sprightly, and enough of a freethinker to become engaged to Franklin's bastard son. However, they could not endure the long separation of his trip to England with his father: they quarreled—probably it was as much her fault as his—and he eventually married someone else. Rebecca Smith made her godmother to her daughter Willy, born while William Smith was in England in 1762, and other friends tried to cheer her; but Miss Graeme declined until a trip of her own to England, where she met the king and flirted with Nathaniel Evans, restored her spirits and determined her to devote her life to the muses. For years thereafter, she conducted Philadelphia's most famous literary salon, translated and retranslated Fénelon's *Telemachus,* and helped Smith edit Evans's literary remains; but her bright and brittle manner showed that she still nursed her wrong, and looked for others to add to it.

Her opportunity came in 1772 when, at the age of thirty-five, she married Henry Hugh Fergusson, a twenty-five-year-old Scotsman recently arrived in America. After three years of marriage, he went to England on business, and only returned to Philadelphia in September, 1777, as a supernumerary of General Sir William Howe.

His agitated wife, living at the family house above Willow Grove, flew to him at once, armed with a pass from Washington, who trusted her and didn't see why she shouldn't cross the lines and visit her husband as often as she chose. She was thus the ideal bearer of Jacob Duché's letter urging Washington to surrender, which she delivered October 15, and which Washington turned over to Congress the next day. Soon after, her husband sent her off on another mission, this time to offer General Joseph Reed £10,000 to defect.

Fergusson was proscribed, and the property of both Fergussons was confiscated by Congress. Reed was asked to intercede for Mrs. Fergusson, and reminded of the literary evenings he had enjoyed at Graeme Park before the war; but he answered that he was under "restraints of a public character which sometimes clash with private feelings." However, Smith organized a large number of her friends, including his brother Thomas, Dr. Rush, John Dickinson, Samuel Powel, Francis Hopkinson, and Thomas Mifflin, and he was able to secure for her, in 1781, the use of her property during her lifetime. Smith and Rebecca Smith remained her friends throughout this disgrace and her subsequent whinings: they wrote her letters, visited her, comforted her, and always showed a special indulgence to the "Laura" of Evans's poems and the translator of *Telemachus*.

In November, 1781, Smith came up to Philadelphia to read the marriage service to Thomas Smith and Letitia Van Deren. Thomas was now thirty-six and, after serving as Assemblyman off and on for years, had lately been elected by Assembly to the Continental Congress. It is fun to think of Thomas Smith galumphing around Independence Hall in his great boots, voting against the National Bank, congratulating everyone in sight on the defeat of Cornwallis, voting to proceed with the congressional investigation of Horatio Gates. It is even more fun to think of William and Thomas together on the wedding day: two big, awkward men poking each other and making the usual jokes, but embellishing them with their thick Scottish accents. The jokes proved apt. Thomas and Letitia had their first child not quite nine months after.

Thomas Smith's marriage cost him his job. Letitia would not move to Bedford, so Smith lost his seat in Assembly, which in turn cost him his seat in Congress. The couple compromised his love of the frontier and her love of civilization by settling in Carlisle, where Smith practiced law until 1791, when he became a Pennsylvania district judge. For William too his brother's marriage was a mixed blessing: he lost his factor in Bedford, but Letitia had some money, which William was soon borrowing from Thomas.

William Smith must have been in Philadelphia again the beginning of June, 1783, for the funeral of his father-in-law. Old Judge Moore was eighty-four when he died, and though he had not tried libeling Assembly again, there is evidence that he remained choleric to the last. He was survived by five of his twelve children, but they and their spouses had to wait another year for their share of his considerable estate (including twelve hundred acres of Chester County land) because he left it all to his wife.

During the nine years that William Smith officially resided in Chestertown, he probably spent no more than half his time there; yet he was able to accomplish a prodigious amount. "You will begin to think by this time [that he] is everywhere, and indeed I think him a most extraordinary compound," Silas Deane wrote of him in 1774; and if anything, his energy increased in the next eight or ten years.

His first job was, as Ezra Stiles put it, his "opulent church living" (six hundred bushels of wheat). The Church of England had been the established church in Maryland from 1702 until 1776, but during the Revolution eighteen of the forty-four Anglican preachers left the state, others died or retired, and none was replaced. Therefore, in 1780 there were twenty preachers for forty-four parishes, no bishops, and no money at all. What was worse, the church was in general disrepute from having been a favorite of the old government. Smith soon came in for his share of the abuse, as when a Baltimore Presbyterian wrote that he hoped his criticism of the Anglicans would not disturb "the Reverend

Dr. S. in his retirement from the world and the things of the world, where he is inhaling copious draughts of sublime contemplation, purifying himself by a course of mental recollection, contrition, and extraordinary devotion for the mitred honors to which he is destined."

Smith called a convention of what was left of the church in Maryland in November, 1780. Only three preachers attended, and twenty-four laymen, mostly from the Eastern Shore, but Smith, as president of the convention, went to work anyway. The name of the church was changed from the Church of England to the Protestant Episcopal Church. A petition was drawn up requesting that Assembly implement a chapter of Maryland's constitution of 1776, allowing it to tax the citizens for the maintenance of religion, though the tax money had to go to whatever sect the citizen chose. The petition was not to be sent to Assembly until approved by all the parishes; but the name of the church was to change immediately, and with no further discussion in Maryland or any other state. That would teach those seventeen other preachers to show up for the next convention!

In addition to the regular Sunday services at Emanuel Church and St. Paul's (when he picked up the other parish is uncertain), Smith was careful to preach special sermons on all the days that Congress set aside. His first sermon in Chestertown was on Tuesday, July 4, 1780. He also preached patriotically on Wednesday, May 23, 1781, when Congress called for a day of fasting, and on Thursday, December 13, 1781, when Congress called for thanksgiving on the surrender of Cornwallis. What with baptisms and burials—and at least a few parish calls, presumably—his ministry would have been a full-time job for a less energetic man.

In January, 1782, he conducted the funeral of

Hugh Neill, who had been his predecessor at Trinity Church, Oxford, and had moved to a church in Wye, farther down the Eastern Shore, in 1766. His mediocre intelligence notwithstanding, Neill had had the wit to recognize that the Maryland oath of fidelity was a direct contradiction of his oath to the church, and the pluck to refuse to take it. However, he had not tried to obstruct the new government, and it had not interfered with him and his remote parish.

Several other conventions of the Maryland Episcopal Church were held, sometimes on the Eastern and sometimes on the Western Shore. Smith usually presided, and a good deal of time was spent discussing the changes that would have to be made in the liturgy to accommodate it to political reality, without offending the church hierarchy in England. The preachers were also anxious to have a hierarchy of their own, and when they were certain that the state of Maryland didn't object, they elected William Smith to be their first bishop, in Annapolis, on August 16, 1783.

A pair of lawn sleeves! He was to have them at last! For more than twenty years he had worked toward that honor in Pennsylvania and now, barely three years after he had come to Maryland as an outcast, the honor was presented to him, almost effortlessly. One difficulty remained: the convention could recommend "our brother, the Rev. Dr. William Smith, as a fit and proper person, and every way well qualified to be invested with the sacred office of a Bishop"; but it would take three English bishops to consecrate him. Samuel Seabury, recommended at about the same time by a Connecticut convention, was two years getting himself consecrated, and wound up having it done by the nonjuring Scottish bishops (i.e., Jacobites who had not sworn allegiance to the house of Hanover, and there-fore did not require Seabury to do so.) Sooner or later, Parliament would have to pass an act allowing English bishops to delete the loyalty oath when consecrating American bishops, and then Smith would be among the first to go over. Meanwhile, he had his letter of recom-mendation from the Maryland convention.

Probably there was very little politicking to Smith's election: he was the natural choice. At that time, there was no other Episcopal preacher of his dis-tinction in Maryland, and perhaps no other in the whole of the thirteen states. He automatically presided at any Maryland convention, and at many national ones too. If he was not noted for theological profundity, nei-ther was his church, and his abilities as an organizer, politician, and propagandist made him particularly well suited to lead a disorganized sect which had lost its political muscle. In addition, he was now principal of the only college in Maryland.

The combination of the Kent County School and Smith's own small academy had, under his leadership, grown to one hundred and forty students by 1782 and he had then persuaded the Board of Visitors to apply to Assembly to add a college onto the school, as had been done with the Academy of Philadelphia. Assembly said yes, but stipulated that the Board must collect at least £5000 before they could make the charter good. At that time, £200,000 was the approximate amount of money circulating in Maryland, but the Board told Smith to go out and get subscriptions for one fortieth of it, and he did it in three months' time.

Smith was then fifty-five years old, compared with the thirty-five he had been when he went collecting for the College of Philadelphia. His trip, made entirely on horseback, was the more difficult because the Eastern Shore is a succession of long peninsulas, and to reach the houses of likely contributors many times he had to backtrack. Of course, old friends helped. William Paca, a graduate of the College of Philadelphia who was now governor of Maryland, did much of the canvassing in Queen Anne county himself, and General Cadwallader, who lived near Chestertown, contributed heavily. By the terms of the appeal, no subscriptions of less than £9 could be accepted. Subscriptions could be paid in three annual installments, in specie or in crops. Any group of people from the same county who subscribed £500 had the right—and their descendants had the perpetual right—to elect a member of the Board of Visitors and Governors. In his three months in the saddle, Smith got subscriptions from three hundred and fifty-four people, and God knows how many others he talked to. Total subscriptions were £6513, worth about £4000 sterling, including £18 of Smith's own money, which must have damn near killed him.

Exhausting as his trip or trips were, Smith must have enjoyed them. Fund raising was one of the things he did best, and in America the rich were not as likely to be guarded by servants and antechambers as they were in England. He liked to talk, to meet people, to show what he could do. And establishing a college would reestablish him in the world as nothing else— not even a bishopric—could do, especially as he meant to call the institution Washington College. The name was included in the act submitted to Assembly in the spring. In July, even before he set out to raise the funds, Smith wrote to Washington, enclosing a copy of the act, informing him that money was already being raised under his name, asking him whether he wouldn't sit on the Board, and implying that a token contribution from him would not be ill received. Oh, yes, and would his excellency come visit sometime soon?

Really, it was very clever of Smith. Once again, he had made it impossible for Washington to refuse, and a month later Washington dictated his reply to Tench Tilghman: "I am much indebted for the honor," etc. Then comes the famous phrase, the phrase which—to this day—some fool in the college alumni office keeps thinking will tickle the fancy and open the wallet of his captive audience: "If the trifling sum of fifty guineas will be considered as an earnest of my wishes for the prosperity of this seminary. . . ." Washington, however, firmly refused to serve on the Board of Visitors and Governors—the war was still going on, and he was too busy.

Smith wrote back ecstatically: "I have by a resolve of the Visitors and Governors of the College, laid out your Present of *Fifty* Guineas in the Purchase of an Elegant *Air-Pump* and some *optical Instruments,* as the Beginning of a Philosophical Apparatus, which we have marked as your Excellency's GIFT to the Seminary." But Washington did not have to answer that letter, and so far as we know, he never did.

Smith's academy students must have been following a college curriculum from the moment he arrived in Chestertown. Otherwise, there is no explaining how he managed to hold the first commencement of Washington College in May, 1783, less than six months after Assembly had received the subscription list which made good the charter. During that winter, three college professors had been holding their classes in the school building; and for commencement Smith mustered a procession and marched to his church. There he awarded degrees to six students, including eighteen-year-old Charles Smith, his third son.

"What a bluster and parade doth the noisy hypocritical Smith make about his son and half a dozen youth?" Ezra Stiles was beside himself when he heard the news. Apparently, Smith had somewhere claimed that this was his third college, and that moved Stiles to write, "As well might the hypocritical Dr. Smith assume upon himself the vanity and absurdity of representing that Harvard and Yale and Dartmouth Colleges were formed on his fictitious model of the College of Mirania as that New York, Philadelphia, and Chester Colleges are. But this is a specimen of his vanity and assuming arrogance. . . . He is an unprincipled turbulent impudent priest. And it is surprising he should take in a number of capital characters in Maryland." In short, Smith had landed on his feet, and Stiles could not forgive him.

The college now had at its disposal over £10,000, counting the £3000 that the school was worth and other monies that had come in since the closing of the subscriptions. The day after commencement, another procession marched out of town and, on a small hill a quarter of a mile from the Chester River, laid the cornerstone of the new college building. Though Smith was the principal functionary—it was his college, wasn't it?—the principal guest was Governor Paca, a member of the Board, who was saluted with thirteen volleys of cannon. There were orations in French, and three students in "shepherds' dresses" delivered a pastoral dialogue (in English, not in bleats).

The brick building, designed by Rakestraw and Hicks of Philadelphia, was to be four storeys high, one hundred and sixty feet long, and sixty feet deep except for the central portion, which was to be one hundred deep. It was to house "near 200 students." It was to be substantially larger than Nassau Hall at Princeton, which was, until that time, the largest building in America. It was to be almost twice the size of "Whitefield's Tabernacle," the building of the College of Philadelphia.

As usual, Smith enjoyed cramming as many events as possible into a few days. While commencement and cornerstone laying were taking place at the college, the Episcopal preachers of Maryland were holding a convention—summoned by Smith—in Chestertown. This had a double advantage for him—it drew the attention of his fellow preachers to the college, and it swelled the ranks of the college processions with distinguished men. The day of the cornerstone laying, while all the church dignitaries were still on hand, Smith married off his oldest daughter Willy to Charles Goldsborough.

It is unlikely that Willy had been any more pleased than her father with the family removal to Maryland. She knew that there would be no *Meschianzas* in Chestertown. The wide, flat river and low shoreline, the monotonous fields, the dark, tangled creeks and hollows, the insignificant towns of the Eastern Shore can hardly have moved a girl who lived for dances and dresses and gossip. After the death of John André, she became engaged to a Dr. Thomas Cradock, a frequenter of her father's Episcopalian conventions. She gave him André's ring, but Cradock was thirty and she was only twenty, and he was inclined to be serious, and she broke it off.

Goldsborough was no picnic either. Tench Tilghman's sister wrote to her cousin in Chestertown, "They say there was never a Jack in the world that could not find a Jill, and truly I am inclined to be of that opinion, since Charles Goldsborough has found one." But Goldsborough was young and rich (his father was a lawyer, sometime Continental Congressman, and a heavy contributor to Washington College), and he may even have been impetuous. Legend says that he tried to get Willy to elope, and once got her "as far as the carriage step" before she decided to hold out for the full ceremony.

For a wedding present, William Smith gave Willy land: eight acres at Falls of Schuylkill, three hundred acres near Huntingdon, twenty-seven hundred and fifty acres in Bedford, and three thousand other acres scattered around northern Pennsylvania and New York. In spite of that, Willy did not have a happy life. Goldsborough took her off to the family plantation near Cambridge, sixty miles further down the Shore, and three years later it was a treat for her to come up to Chestertown for a visit. She bore Goldsborough four children, and died of it.

William sent the newly graduated Charles to Carlisle to study law with his Uncle Thomas—a peculiar decision, as Thomas had no formal legal training himself. Thomas wrote, "I trust I have it in my power to return some small part of the great obligation I am under to the father, through the son." Charles was an independent youngster, of romantic taste, as can be seen from his trigonometry and surveying notebook, full of lovely little watercolor sketches of trees and castles.

Smith now had two children left at home: Richard, fourteen and a student at the college, and Becky, his favorite daughter, now eleven years old. William Moore Smith, the eldest son, was practicing law in Easton

*David Rittenhouse by Charles Willson Peale*

*Benjamin Franklin,*
*wood sculpture by William Rush*

*Benjamin Rush,*
*by W. R. Jones*
*after a drawing*
*by W. Haines*

(where he could watch over his father's Northampton County real estate) and composing a book of mediocre poetry, which he published three years later. Thomas Duncan Smith was a doctor, and William had settled him in Huntingdon. He could practice medicine anywhere, so why shouldn't he keep an eye on the proprietorship at the same time?

After the Revolution, the Huntingdon town lots sold better, though the provision that each purchaser build a house within a year of settlement was hard to enforce. When most of the original lots were sold, Smith divided up more land into "out-lots," which he also sold, or rather leased, so that he could collect quit-rents forever. He applied the same system to the land surrounding Washington College—selling ninety-nine-year leases to building lots—but to dispose of them quickly, he organized a kind of sales party, dispensed five gallons of rum, and knocked down sixty-three lots.

Rum was also portioned out to the workers on the college building, but Smith took his own earnings in cash: £500 a year, out of an academic payroll of about £1800. Casting about for more money, he got permission from Assembly to organize a college lottery, and wrote to Washington to see whether he wouldn't like to sell some tickets. After all, he was out of the army by that time, and might be looking for something to do. Washington answered that a Mr. Ariss of Alexandria might dispose of two or three hundred, out of the 100,000 that Smith had had printed.

Smith began a new subscription, this time accepting contributions of any size, though those under £3 were to be paid quickly. To inform and encourage donors, he published *An Account of Washington College,* with a preamble in his most florid style: "In that extent of territory which, through the Providence of God, is now the sovereign domain of the United States of America. . . ." Also included were the Assembly's act for founding the college, a list of the original subscribers, Smith's correspondence with Washington, and a chart of the curriculum, which was identical with the College of Philadelphia, "with the addition of such books, instruments, etc., as the many late discoveries and improvements in the Arts and Sciences render necessary." Smith concluded with three pages of prayers, to guide "such of the Masters as are desirous of being assisted with a short form; while every Master is left at his pleasure to add to the same, or to pray without a form, according to his religious persuasion."

George Washington did finally visit the college in May, 1784, almost two years after his first invitation; and we can only guess what strings Smith pulled to get him there. *Gustavus Vasa* was decorously performed by the students—the Philadelphia performance the year before had been "as much like a Bull-beat as a play. Noise, shouting, and ill manners of every kind and denomination, was all the entertainment," said Smith. In Chestertown, the play was followed by an occasional epilogue, spoken by the student but composed by Smith, linking Vasa and Washington:

> How long did fell oppression, o'er this land,
> With more than *Danish Fury* raise her hand;
> When lo! a hero of immortal name
> From where Potowmack rolls his mighty stream,
> Arose the champion of his country's cause;
> The friend of mankind, liberty, and laws. . . .

Washington must have gotten this kind of sycophancy everywhere he went, and it is remarkable that, in the face of it, he remained so plain and decent a man. He allowed himself to be placed on the Board of Visitors and Governors, which, according to law, required him to attend at least one meeting a year or else forfeit his seat. There is no record of his having visited the college again, but he remained on the Board until 1789, when his election as president gave him the excuse to resign.

The finances of the college improved in 1785 when Assembly passed a bill to found St. John's College in Annapolis and to make it and Washington College the two campuses of the University of Maryland. It was implicit in the charter of Washington College that it was to be, in some manner, a state institution, but now that it was explicit, the college began to receive £1250 a year in state support. Smith became a member of the University Board, and an official canvasser for funds for St. John's (along with a popish priest and the Presbyterian who had derided his "mitred honors" from Baltimore), but St. John's didn't get off the ground for five years, and the state university never did.

The Bishop-elect of Maryland became, after his election, an even greater attender of church conventions than before. The following June he went down to a Maryland convention in Annapolis, where he preached the opening sermon and presided over the subsequent meeting. A strong resolution was passed to "keep the bishop in his place." He was to be allowed to confirm, ordain, and consecrate, and to preside over meetings, but aside from that his power was to "differ in nothing from that of other priests." It was a slap in the face, but it was the worst they could do to him, or so it seemed.

He went up to New York that fall to the first general convention ever held by the Protestant Episcopal Church—sixteen preachers and eleven laymen from nine states. Smith was the sole representative from Maryland, but was chosen president of the convention, and helped shepherd through a general ecclesiastical constitution. The whole thing was a triumph for him —his life seemed a long succession of triumphs these days—except for one small hitch: he got more than usually drunk at the convention, or so it seemed to at least one of the delegates (presumably William White), who reported what he had seen to Rev. John Andrews. Well, what of it? Who was Andrews anyhow, to think that he could make an issue of it?

John Andrews was then thirty-eight years old. A classmate of White's at the College of Philadelphia, he had—like Smith—divided his adult life between preaching and teaching, but with much more modest success. He had taught at the Academy of Philadelphia and at Lancaster and York, Pennsylvania, and had held churches at York, at Lewes, Delaware, and on the Eastern Shore. He was currently rector of a church in Baltimore. He is not known to have had any personal grudges against Smith.

A further meeting of the Maryland church was held the end of October, and money was collected to send the Bishop-elect to England for consecration as soon as the English bishops agreed to it. It seemed that Smith was not in any trouble, but just to be on the safe side, he gave John Andrews an honorary D.D. at the 1785 commencement of Washington College.

The next general convention, held in Philadelphia in September, 1785, and presided over by William White, was chiefly concerned with a problem that had been discussed several times in the Maryland conventions: how to reconcile the liturgy of the Church of England with the political exigencies of the Protestant Episcopal Church in America. Obviously, the prayer for the king must be amended, and in the catechism the answer to the question "What is thy duty toward thy neighbor?" could no longer be "To honor and obey the king, to submit myself" etc. But were other changes also indicated? Perhaps the new political liberty called for new religious liberty too. Smith was made chairman of a committee to consider a thorough revision of the prayer book.

Meeting after convention hours, Smith's committee worked out the draft of a new prayer book with many small changes—the committeemen must have been thinking about them for years—and several major ones. The Athanasian and Nicene creeds were to be omitted entirely and the words "He descended into hell" were to be struck out of the remaining creed. It was a logical extension of Episcopalian thought: if none of *us* must go to hell, why must *Jesus?*

The convention approved most of the committee's changes, and used the revised forms for its closing service, at which Smith preached the sermon. He and White and another preacher prepared the book for the press, but when it came out, in April, 1786, it so shocked the English bishops that one of them wrote, "While the church's interests are in such hands as Dr. Smith's, there is no great ground to hope for much good to her." They refused to consecrate American bishops until it was revised.

What remains of William Smith's alterations to the Episcopal prayerbook is the preface. It is in his best, simplest style, and is mellifluous and delightful to read —the sentences long but strongly structured, with the pauses in thought miraculously conforming to breadth and vision. The substance is particularly appealing too: religion is eternal, but the forms of worship are not, and should be adjusted to suit times and places. The church, and even the English bishops, let him get away with saying that much.

When the general convention met in October, 1786, it had just learned that the English bishops were now, by act of Parliament, allowed to consecrate three American bishops, and Smith applied to be one, showing his 1783 election paper. This paper the convention refused to honor, and it chose Provoost of New York, White of Pennsylvania, and Griffith of Virginia to be its three bishops—in addition to Seabury of Connecticut, who had recently returned from Scotland with his lawn sleeves.

Smith went to the Maryland convention, two weeks later, loaded for bear. Between the two conventions, he got a letter from his Chestertown vestry attesting to his "purity of manners." He also had his election paper of three years before: enough evidence to blast any lying rumors that might be circulating about him.

The minutes of the Maryland convention have disappeared: it is more than coincidence how many documents damaging to Smith are no longer to be found. In this case, Smith may have had the chance to destroy them himself, or William White—who was fond of him and didn't want to hurt him, even though he didn't want a drunken bishop in his church—may have destroyed them for him. In any case, what happened at the convention is readily seen from the subsequent correspondence of the delegates.

Smith arrived late. Thomas Cradock, Willy's discarded suitor, was first to speak to him on the subject, but Smith was adamant. After all the years he had been drinking, why was such a big fuss being made about it now? And anyway, who was to say where social drinking ended and drunkenness began? He hadn't fallen down this time, had he? He'd have the matter out before the whole convention. Cradock was making altogether too much out of a little malicious gossip John Andrews had sent him. Smith insisted that his vestry recommendation be read into the minutes, and demanded that his election be reconfirmed.

The convention took the matter up reluctantly: all the delegates knew him well, and knew what he had done to put their church back on its feet after the Revolution. With great respect and politeness, they rose, one after another, to tell what they had heard about his being "much intoxicated, when at New York." It appeared that Andrews was not the only informant: at least two other sources were cited, and at last one of the delegates who had signed the original paper requested that his name be struck off it, "which D.S. refused, as the charge was not made out." But the charge was indeed made out: the lawn sleeves slipped from Smith's arms before he had rightly put them on, and never again—even by Smith—was it suggested that he wear them. His only satisfaction was to go home with his election paper—with no names crossed out—and keep it with him till he died. Damn it, he *had* been elected.

# 8 ❀ Restoration

Fortunately for William Smith, the bishopric was not his only iron in the fire. His town of Huntingdon continued to grow, particularly after the creation of Huntingdon county in 1787, when it became a county seat. That year alone, Smith sold the leases to thirty-four lots —many of them, presumably, to aspirants for county jobs. By the next year, the tax assessment showed fifty-four houses, one hundred and fifty-five leased lots, four stills, and one brewery. The population was at least five hundred in town, and thousands in the surrounding countryside.

To the new government Smith gave land for a courthouse and jail, but the county was in such chaos that, even had the buildings been built at once, they would hardly have sufficed. In March, 1788, country militiamen swarmed into town, carrying an effigy of their colonel and claiming that his election had been rigged. When the sheriff tried to arrest the ringleader, friends prevented it, and a riot ensued.

When tempers seemed to have cooled, Thomas Duncan Smith, who was now a magistrate as well as a doctor, issued warrants against the ringleaders, but on the day of trial they entirely filled the courtroom with their following and demanded that they be locked up. As the jail was nothing but a log cabin, and as they clearly meant to destroy it, Smith refused. They then insulted him, threatened him with a cutlass, and stamped out.

In the afternoon they came back, ninety strong, called Smith out into the square, poked him with the muzzle of a rifle, and demanded that he tear up their warrants. He refused, but allowed them to take the warrants from his pocket and tear them up themselves. "See now what it is to be a magistrate!" they shouted, throwing the scraps in his face. They then terrified the clerk of the court into bringing out the docket, from which they obliterated all mention of themselves; and Smith, the sheriff, and the constables had to hide out until the rioters left town. "Thus ended this unhappy affair," Smith wrote to Benjamin Franklin, who had come home from France for the last time and was now President of Pennsylvania. "The sheriff dares not go into the country to serve any writs, and all kinds of business seems at a stand."

Two months later, William Smith was in Huntingdon to check the figures of the tax assessor, but he evidently took the cash and left the government to his son. The same year, he bought from the estate of George Croghan 27,300 acres near Bedford. The payment was only £100, but as the contract was written ten years earlier, it is likely that this was final rather than full payment. It made him the owner of about thirty-six thousand acres around Bedford, or fifty-six square miles, and about thirty-four thousand acres in other places, or well over one hundred square miles in all—not an enor-

mous holding for a land baron, but still a tidy parcel
for a preacher to put together from scratch. From that
time onward, he bought less land than he gave away to
his children, though in some cases he reserved the income of the gifts to himself during his lifetime.

Smith was also busy trying to get his College of
Philadelphia back from those "robbers," the Trustees
of the University of the State of Pennsylvania. The robbers had included General Joseph Reed, sometime
member of Smith's literary circle of thirty years before,
who had, as President of Pennsylvania in 1779, pushed
the bill that took the College away from Smith and the
old trustees. They had also included Rittenhouse,
Dickenson, William White, Ewing, Hopkinson,
Thomas Mifflin, General Cadwallader—nearly every
friend and every enemy that Smith had had in his adult
life. Increasingly, as the years went by, he realized that
his hope of restoration lay in the state government, and
to it rather than to the trustees he directed his appeals.

Smith's petition to the Council of Censors was re-
jected in 1784, but not until there had been a better
debate on it than at any time in the last five years. That
autumn, Smith again petitioned Assembly, and he was
only defeated when a group of his old enemies bolted
from the chamber, leaving it without a quorum. However, it was a moral victory, and it set the stage for
1788.

Smith prepared Assembly with a published *Address to the General Assembly of Pennsylvania in the
Case of the Violated Charter of the College.* "The constitution of Pennsylvania directs the legislature to nurse
and encourage seminaries of learning, but not to destroy them," he says. He gives a history of the College,

quotes the act that has cost him his living, and says that he hopes soon to insert in the College register or carve on the front of Whitefield's Tabernacle the same sentence that was used at Queen's College, Oxford, after its restoration by William of Orange: "By divine assistance, mercy, and providence, this college, rescued from worse than Babylonian captivity, was restored to its entire and legitimate membership. . . ."

For himself, Smith wants no more than justice: his £250 salary, plus £200 a year for not having the use of the provost's house, or £4400 for eight years, "besides interest, justly due him, out of the funds which he created, and which hath been bestowed upon another man, under whom the seminary has neither increased in reputation nor usefulness, but is said to have been devoted more to political and party cabals, than to the advancement of sound and real literature."

Trying to make it sound as if only Ewing and the trustees stand against him, Smith says that Benjamin Franklin "hath never forgotten his first love, namely the College, Academy, and Charitable School of Philadelphia." Actually, Franklin had never forgotten his old grudge, and he wrote, shortly after Assembly's decision, his *Observations Relative to the Intentions of the Original Founders of the Academy of Philadelphia,* charging that the English school at the Academy had been sacrificed to the Latin school, and practical to classical education. There is little basis for this charge. The English school in Philadelphia continued to flourish under Smith and Washington College also offered strong practical education, as well as the classics. It is only that, in both places, the less worldly studies were considered to be more advanced, more academically distinguished, and they were more touted. At commencement, for example, the valedictory was more likely to be on Plato's *Republic* than on bookkeeping. However, with the deification of Franklin, this last slander of Smith has become sacrosanct; and like any divine text, it can no longer be confuted by reason.

The bill before Assembly was an act to repeal parts of the 1779 act. Many people besides Franklin—we may be sure that Ewing was one of them—tried to block it, but it was a matter of muscle now, not of argument. Franklin had lost most of his following in the many years he had been away, and though he was President of the Supreme Executive Council of Pennsylvania until 1789 and was accorded every honor until the day he died, he had little power left. Even had he not been eighty-two years old and wracked with the set of infirmities that formed the chief topic of his correspondence in his last years, his party was generally in retreat. In 1787 he and Rittenhouse were candidates for the state ratifying convention of the federal constitution, and were defeated five to one, and in 1790 the state constitution he had helped write was replaced by a far less radical one.

In Assembly, it was clearly going to be Smith's day. He came up from Maryland, and on the morning that the repealing vote was to be taken, a doctor friend of Ewing's approached an Assemblyman and asked that a rider be attached to the bill, specifying that the University should not be accountable for its use of the College money and property during the interregnum. Smith was shown the rider, and he wrote:

THE RIDER

On mischief bent, by Ewing sent,
  With *Rider* in his hands,

Comes Doctor GUTS, with mighty struts,
  And thus of Smith demands:

"This Rider, sir, to save all stir,
  By Master Ewing's will,
I bring in haste, pray get some paste,
  And tack it on your Bill."

Smith lifts his eyes—"Hoot! mon," he cries,
  "Take back your stupid stuff,
Our answer's brief, the crafty thief
  Had *ridden* lang enuff."

The bill passed Assembly on March 6, 1789. All buildings and funds that had been theirs in 1779 were restored to the old trustees and faculty, and gaps in their ranks were quickly filled: the professorship in moral philosophy, for example, was awarded to Rev. John Andrews. The Board met March 9 at Franklin's house (he was too weak to go out), and as Smith wrote piously in the minutebook, they elected as their president "the Venerable Dr. Benjamin Franklin, the father and one of the first founders of the institution."

With his restoration as provost of the College of Philadelphia (and his restoration to the provost's house —Ewing had to move out) Smith prepared to give up his Maryland connections. However, there were too many ties to cut them all at once, and some of them might be useful a little longer. George Washington, for instance, had just resigned from the Board of Washington College, and it seemed a good opportunity to give him a Doctor of Laws degree. To make sure that he couldn't refuse, Smith and two Board members, both Congressmen, gave it to him in New York, where the federal government was then doing business. Once again, Washington was buffaloed, and he wrote cour-

teously to Smith, "It affords me peculiar pleasure to
know that the seat of learning under your direction
hath attained such proficiency. . . ."

At Washington College commencement that year,
Smith presided for the last time. The huge building
had been dedicated the year before, and Thomas Smith
had come down for the party and given thirty shillings
to help pay the musicians, but a year later the building
was still only structurally complete, and it really never
did get finished.

The family had to be moved back to the city. For
Mrs. Smith, it was a return to her friends and the place
where she had grown up. For Willy, who remained
with her husband in Cambridge, it meant that she now
had less reason to go to Chestertown, and was that
much more cut off from the world she loved. For Richard, who had graduated from Washington College and
was now studying law, probably in Philadelphia, the
move cannot have much mattered. But for Becky, who
was now seventeen and had lived in Chestertown since
she was eight, the move was very sad. She was "the vic-
tim of despair," wrote one of her gossipy friends. "Sunday evening she paid me a farewell visit. After half an
hour's pensive, sentimental conversation in the piano
tone, she gave me a tender embrace, hung her head,"
etc. There is no gossipist to tell us how Primus, a favorite slave whom the Smiths took back to Philadelphia,
felt about the move.

Even after he charged his last class of graduates
and left Chestertown, William Smith kept his interest
in Washington College, probably as a member of the
Board, though there are no records. He came back for
at least one more commencement, in May, 1790. In November, 1789, he preached the sermon at the opening

of St. John's College, and was elected President *pro tempore* of the Board. He was at that time a delegate from Washington College to the anticipated convocation of the University of Maryland; and thus he was, for a moment anyway, an important official of three colleges and one university.

The projected University of Maryland never got off the ground, because Washington College never sent enough members to its board meetings to make a quorum. St. John's, after a slow start, grew fairly steadily, and even survived the act by which Assembly cut off support to both Maryland colleges in 1805. But Washington College, without Smith to drive it, quickly fell prey to the lassitude and anti-intellectualism that have characterized the Eastern Shore from its first settlement to the present day. La Rochefoucalt-Liancourt, who visited it in 1796, said, "Panes are lacking in all the windows, the walls are cracked in many places, there are no stairs at the doorways. . . . It maintains a president and three masters who are said to be good; but the number of students isn't more than forty or fifty. . . . Like almost all public buildings in America, it falls in ruins before it is finished." The state subsidy was cut off in 1805, and in 1827 the building burnt to the ground, and everything was lost—furniture, books, papers, and George Washington's elegant air pump. A handful of determined people—fanatics, they must have been—kept the college alive through the nineteenth century.

The College of Philadelphia, after its restoration, had buildings, trustees, faculty, and an endowment of perhaps £20,000. What it did not have was students, for Ewing and his trustees, instead of closing the University, moved it first to the Masonic Hall, and then to

the new building of the American Philosophical Society. The State House adjoined, which was convenient
for Ewing, who was allowed to summon his students by
ringing the Liberty Bell. Smith, to get students, re-
sorted to advertisements in the newspapers. By July, he
had collected "near one hundred scholars, which are
daily increasing," as a Philadelphian wrote Ezra Stiles,
and Stiles wrote in his diary, "Dr. Smith is a haughty,
self-opinionated, half-learned character."

Smith was not necessarily content to let the two institutions continue, side by side. Perhaps, he wrote to a
friend, the University had no right to exist, now that
the act that created it had been repealed. Certainly the
money with which the state had endowed the University was rightfully the money of the College, and he
meant to sue for it, if necessary. And how about the
money he himself was owed by the University or College or perhaps both—how about the £4400, plus interest? The repeal bill hadn't even mentioned that.

Smith got back into the swing of his Philadelphia
life right away—really, he had never been out of it,
what with his commuting from Chestertown. In August he published a pamphlet, "Proposals for printing
by subscription, a body of sermons upon the most important branches of practical Christianity," with two
blank leaves at the end where subscribers could sign
up. He continued to attend the meetings of the American Philosophical Society, and for its records observed a
transit of Mercury from Chestertown in November (he
was on his way to preach his sermon at St. John's) while
Rittenhouse observed it in Philadelphia. In January,
he, Rittenhouse, and Ewing—damn the man, he was
everywhere—were elected vice-presidents of the society.

But Smith's life was not entirely pleasure during

his first year back in the city: his son, Thomas Duncan Smith, died in July at the age of twenty-eight. He had continued to live in Huntingdon, doing his best to restrain the rioters, in whom dislike for their militia colonel was entangled with dislike for the new federal constitution. At least once his house had been stoned, and there had been talk of tarring and feathering him. He died of fever, worn out from his two jobs as doctor and magistrate—and also from the effort he must have put into looking after his father's real estate.

At Christmastime, Smith's wife Rebecca very nearly died of pleurisy. She recovered, but was never really in good health again, and probably had not been for some time before.

One death that cannot have disturbed him too much was Franklin's, on April 17, 1790. It would have disturbed him even less if he could have read Franklin's unpublished pamphlet of the year before, in which he compared studying the classics to wearing a *chapeau bras* and recommended a separation of English and Latin schools, "but claiming an equitable partition of our joint stock."

With enormous pomp, Franklin's body was borne to its simple grave, beside the wife he had devoted so much of his energy to cheating on. The pallbearers included David Rittenhouse, Philadelphia Mayor Samuel Powel, and Pennsylvania President Mifflin and Chief Justice McKean. Smith had dinner with the pallbearers at Mifflin's house at the Falls, but he marched far back in the funeral procession; and many people were surprised when the American Philosophical Society, voting on who should deliver the formal eulogy, split evenly between him and Rittenhouse.

Politics had little to do with the vote that Smith

got. Though he was Franklin's enemy, he had known the old man longer and better than anyone else then living, except perhaps William Franklin, who was now proscribed. Also, he was still the best public speaker in Philadelphia, and perhaps in the whole of America. Rittenhouse, on the other hand, had been Franklin's close friend and political ally the few times they had both been in the city in the last twenty years; but Rittenhouse was a poor writer and a really abysmal speaker. It was months—during which each man refused to take precedence over the other—before Smith agreed to deliver the Franklin eulogy, provided Rittenhouse would help him prepare the scientific portion.

The eulogy, delivered the following March, was attended by the entire Philosophical Society membership, the entire state and federal governments (including George Washington, of course), and all the Philadelphia printers. Glorying in the eulogistic form, Smith broke forth at once: "Citizens of Pennsylvania! Luminaries of science! Assembled Fathers of America! Heard you not the solemn interrogatory? Who is *he* who now recedes from his labors among you? What citizen, supereminent in council, do you now deplore? What luminary, what splendid son of science, from the hallowed walks of philosophy, now withdraws his beams? What father of his country, what hero, what statesman, what law-giver, is now extinguished from your political hemisphere, and invites the mournful obsequies? Is it *he*—your FRANKLIN? It cannot be!"

The body of the eulogy, when Smith got down to it, was largely about Franklin's rise in the world, his philanthropies in Philadelphia, and his scientific discoveries. It did not touch on Pennsylvania political disputes, because "he who now addresses you was too much an actor in the scene to be fit for the discussion of it"; nor his services to America while abroad, which were "too well known." Smith then said he had proof that Franklin believed in immortality (Franklin would have been tickled by that), and closed with another burst of rhetoric, this time addressing not the audience but the dead man: "Yes, thou dear departed friend and fellow-citizen! Thou, too, art gone before us—thy chair, thy celestial car, was first ready! We must soon follow, and we know where to find thee! May we seek to follow thee by lives of virtue and benevolence like thine . . . ."

Horace Wemyss Smith tells a little story that should finish off any discussion of William Smith and Benjamin Franklin. "Oh, Papa," said Becky Smith when her father got home from delivering the eulogy, "I don't think you believed more than one-tenth part of what you said of old Ben Lightning-rod. Did you?" Smith laughed, but did not answer.

Smith was much in demand as a speaker: he preached to the Society of the Cincinnati when the Fourth of July fell on a Sunday, and he prepared and personally read to attentive Brother Washington an address from the Grand Lodge of Pennsylvania, full of the usual Masonic rubbish about terrestrial and celestial lodges, cherubim and seraphim, etc. For some reason— perhaps for brevity—the White Stone and the Three Orders did not figure in the address.

In July, 1790, Charles Smith presented himself to the Trustees of the College of Philadelphia and asked to be taken on as a lecturer in law. Charles had been practicing in Sunbury for the last four years, and look- ing after his father's Northumberland County real estate at the same time. There had already been talk of start- ing law courses at the College, but Charles's letter brought it to a head; and as a result, in August, the trustees appointed James Wilson, one of their own number, their first law professor.

Charles must have been disappointed, but he had now been in the civilized parts of Pennsylvania for nearly a year, what with being a Northumberland delegate to the state constitutional convention, and he showed little inclination to go back to the boondocks. In September, he got himself engaged to Mary Yeates of Lancaster, and after he married her, he moved to her town, rather than move her to his. What, Lancaster? William Smith didn't own any property in Lancaster! Hadn't he given the boy three thousand acres of outlands and even two lots in Huntingdon town, to let him know where his interest lay? And who was going to manage the western lands if not Charles? True, Richard had finished his law training and been settled in Huntingdon soon after Thomas Duncan died there, but Richard wasn't all that stable a character. Before there was any talk of Charles's moving, his father had written, "He is justly a favorite son, and has never in his life, by any part of his conduct, given me cause of pain, but always of much pleasure." What could the boy be thinking of now?

In December, 1790, Willy died at the age of twenty-eight. She was the second of Smith's grown children to die in less than two years. In a tardy letter to her husband, he wrote, "Inconsolable myself, unmanned, and I fear almost *unchristianed,* with the mother, sister and brothers of the angel we have lost, all in the like condition around me, what consolation could I impart to you?" He sent a tutor down for her two little boys, and he ordered carved on her gravestone:

Called from this mortal scene in bloom of life,
Here lies a much lov'd daughter, mother, wife,
To whom each grace and excellence were given,
A saint on earth, an angel now in heaven. . . .

Willy was no saint or angel, of course, but we cannot blame William Smith for thinking so, or for wishing that she had been.

In January, 1791, the trustees of the College wrote a letter to the trustees of the University, saying that they understood the University was considering union, and that the College would be willing to consider their suggestions. The University trustees wrote back that the idea certainly did not originate with them, but that now that it was broached, they would entertain it. After a little more sparring, two committees got down to the bargaining that summer.

Until at least a hundred years after that time, there was no need for two colleges in Philadelphia. The population of the city had hardly built up to what it had been before the Revolution, and was soon to be decimated again by yellow fever. Dividing the money, the students, and the teaching talent in half was disastrous, though it was the money pinch that was felt first: both institutions were now in debt, and Philadelphians were not in a mood to give to either. During and immediately after the Revolution, there had been intense interest in education in almost every state, and many colleges were founded. But the same change in public feeling that allowed Maryland Assembly to cut down and finally cut off support to Washington College, made it economically impossible for the College of Philadelphia and the University to continue their rivalry, which was more than anything a rivalry between Smith and Ewing.

Smith did not have a lot to say about the merger. Though he kept the minutes of the Board, he was not a trustee, and could not vote in its decisions. He was not a president. He was only a provost (which was also all that Ewing was, across the street), and as such he was a teacher, the "principal officer of the faculty," and he had certain other taxing but not particularly distinguishing tasks, such as overseeing the students and the College property. It is hard to tell whether he had as much suasion over the restored Board as he had had over the earlier one: probably not. At any rate, he may not have opposed the union, for the final document was written in his own hand. He may have thought he was going to be provost of the whole shebang.

The compromise, as worked out by the two committees and passed by Assembly in September, named the new institution the University of Pennsylvania. Each of the old boards was to elect twelve members to the new one, and the faculty—for it was certain that there were to be some cuts—was to be chosen by the new board "from each institution equally." All buildings and funds were of course to be combined.

The new board met in November, and it soon coalesced enough to decide that the funds would support but six professors—natural philosophy, moral philosophy, mathematics, English and belles lettres, German and oriental languages, and classical languages. Smith was well equipped to teach five of the six, but Ewing of the old University was quickly elected to the first job, and John Andrews of the old College to the second. So the jobs went, one after another, but with increasing bitterness at each election, until in April, 1792, James

Davidson, who had been teaching the classics at the College for twenty years, off and on, was elected to the last one. We may be sure that David Rittenhouse, a trustee brought over from the old University, was one of the thirteen who voted for Davidson, not one of the eleven who voted for Smith. Not long after, Ewing was elected provost and Andrews vice-provost of the new University.

Almost exactly on his sixty-fifth birthday, William Smith was—in effect—fired a second time from a college he had helped found. At least, the trustees thought they had fired him. Smith wasn't so sure, and he wrote them on April 16, asking "whether after 40 years in the seminary, they considered me, by any act of theirs, absolved or discharged from further duties in it, and on what terms. . . ."

The trustees appointed a committee to look into Smith's claims, and when they met again, ten days later, they were confronted by a far more menacing letter. His £100 was for *life,* he said, and suggested that the provost's house really ought to be his for life too, especially as he had just spent $200 on making it "convenient and comfortable to his family." Anyway, he couldn't be removed from his job "by any change of name or other circumstance, but [only] by his own *declining* or *resigning* it. . . . Nor can any new professor be chosen, while any of the old are *alive* and *willing to serve.*" His arguments were "founded on principles of *justice* and *equity.* How far they are founded in *law* also, I trust there will never be occasion to enquire.

"If it be the opinion of the Trustees that my services can be spared for a time, without injury to the seminary, till a final establishment of its funds shall take place, and saving to myself my own rights, it is in my power during the ensuing summer, to be of some public service in another way, although neither equally agreeable nor advantageous to myself. . . . While I shall be spared by you the drudgery of teaching, I shall have no objection to suffer a reasonable part of my former salary to go to those who are employed in actual service. . . . The circumstances of my family are such that the use of the house, and a residence in the city, is absolutely necessary."

The trustees tabled the letter. In November, when they had cooled down enough to consider it again, they resolved to continue his annuity, and to let him use the house rent free until the next April.

When Smith spoke of "public service in another way," he may have meant political office. The preceding fall, he had written to the speaker of the state senate, offering himself as a candidate for United States senator. More likely he meant the writing of a *History of the American Revolution.* In a letter to George Washington, written two weeks after his ouster from the University, he asked to be given the use of state papers, and Washington answered that he could see any unclassified ones. However, the book was never written, and the Senate seat never proffered.

While waiting to find out whether he had a job, Smith exerted himself again for Elizabeth Graeme Fergusson, and was able to help her secure the right to sell her family estate, Graeme Park. "Cannot you spare a couple of days?" she wrote to Mrs. Smith, when the place was sold but she had not yet moved out. "Could not you and Mrs. Bond and Mrs. Hopkinson and your little granddaughter come up in your carriages and pay a last solitary visit? My beds are as yet in *status quo* and also my furniture." She was still trying to defend herself to Philadelphia for being a Loyalist and to her husband (whom she had not seen for fourteen years) for being a revolutionary, and she was hoping that Mrs. Smith would deliver testimonials behind doors that were closed to her. Mrs. Fergusson had become a really nauseating woman, and signed her letter, "Your much injured friend."

The purchaser of Graeme Park was Rev. William Smith. Almost before he had moved the last occupant out, he had a chance to sell it, but set a price that would have "very amply compensated me," and the purchaser backed off. He then leased it out on good terms to "a couple of good industrious Germans." Mrs. Fergusson lived out her days in a hotel called "the Billet."

In May, Becky Smith married Samuel Blodget, a widower with five children. In spite of being a wiseacre, Becky wanted to make a good marriage of it, and twice wrote to Benjamin Rush to ask his advice. "Try to *do* as well as *say* clever things," the sober Rush advised her. In concluding the second letter, he wrote, "Imitate your excellent mother, as far as her situation in life resembles yours, and your late excellent sister." Then he thought about that sentence and deleted it from the final draft.

Becky's marriage with Blodget was not happy. He was in the East India trade, and in land speculation, and traveled about a lot. In addition, he beat her so often that she finally left him and took a series of lovers. At forty-three, "Mrs. B was exactly in person, manner, and conversation what she was when 18 years old," said Rush, unconsciously echoing what William Smith had said about Jacob Duché: "the same at 36 that he was at 18." Then Rush added a series of adjectives that were purely his own, and purely about Becky: "Beautiful, sprightly, eloquent, sensible, imprudent, desultory, and censorious."

Now that Smith was well out of Maryland, and could not possibly claim the right to the bishopric there, a Maryland convention chose Thomas Claggett in his place. Claggett was twenty years younger than Smith, and he undoubtedly enjoyed other advantages as well. In a gesture that was no doubt meant to be kind, but that must have piqued as much as it pleased, Smith was given precedence over the three consecrating bishops, and was allowed to preach the sermon.

He departed from a standard text at several points, once to say that his long friendship with Claggett, "as well as other good considerations, render it unnecessary for me to say much. . . ." There must have been many in the church who remembered that Claggett had joined Cradock and the others to put down Smith's own episcopal ambitions at the Maryland convention five years before. A little later in his sermon, Smith mentioned "the station which I have chosen to hold in the church during the short remaining span of my life." The hearts of many listeners—among them Bishop White—must really have been in their mouths, for Smith was perfectly capable of airing his whole grievance anew, but he wisely passed on to more conventional things, and the day was saved.

1793 will always be remembered in Philadelphia as the year of the plague. Yellow fever had visited the city before—a good many cases were recorded in the 1740's, and a pesthouse was built to contain them. Hundreds died in the epidemic of 1762, but then the Dock Creek —really an open sewer—was arched over and filled. After that the disease was not a major problem until

1793, when it was brought to the city on ships carrying refugees from the revolution in Haiti, and spread by the local mosquitoes, especially numerous that summer. Benjamin Rush noted his first cases the beginning of August, and by the 19th he was calling it an epidemic.

Dr. Rush was forty-seven at that time: an eminent practitioner, a signer of the Declaration of Independence, a professor of chemistry and medicine at the College since 1768. "Observation without principles is nothing but empiricism. . . . It is by means of *principles* in medicine that a physician can practice with safety to his patients, and satisfaction to himself." As good as his word, in the beginning of September Rush decided that some coffee rotting on the wharf was responsible for the plague in Philadelphia, and he prescribed awesome blood lettings and "mercurial sweating purges." Once reasoned and prescribed, these remedies could not be disproved with mere evidence, and by the force of his personality Rush got most Philadelphia doctors to go along with him.

One man, more than any other, stood out in opposition—Stephen Girard, the one-eyed French businessman who gave up his work to take over the fever lazaretto, and who dared to say, "The pernicious treatment of our doctors sent many of our citizens to another world." Having known yellow fever as a young man in the Caribbean, he wanted it treated with quinine, a light diet, and rest. "By leading a regular life, it is possible to live here in good health." Unfortunately for the Smiths, their family doctor was Benjamin Rush.

In that curiously lost diary that Horace Wemyss Smith claimed his great-grandfather kept, notice of the plague began appearing August 28. By that time, the death rate was already over twenty a day, and everybody who had someplace to go was getting out of town. A week later, most of the federal and state government was gone from Philadelphia, though part of the cabinet was reassembled and trying to do business in Germantown. On September 10, Washington left for Mt. Vernon, and Smith wrote in his diary, "We still stay in our town-house, as I consider it my duty as a clergyman to remain where I can be of some consolation and use." Indeed, he might as well make the best of it: after Alexander Hamilton caught the fever, Comptroller Wolcott moved what was left of the Treasury Department out to Smith's house at the Falls.

The yellow fever was at its height from September 15 to October 15, with deaths averaging seventy a day, though some days they were over one hundred. "We daily burn gunpowder about the house, and Primus makes smoke in the cellar," Smith had written September 10. "Dr. Rush calls on us every day, and for some days gives us gentle doses of salts; but he now advises the use of barks, or of calomel and jalap. In fact, he knows not what to give." By the end of the month, Rush was making no social calls: with heroism to match his wrongheadedness, he was treating at least one hundred patients a day, and dooming hundreds more with his advice in the one remaining newspaper. His energy was the more remarkable in that he suffered his first attack of the fever on September 15, and what with recurrences and the devastations of his own remedies, he was never well again, as long as the plague lasted.

On September 29, he added to his list of dead patients Samuel Powel, the gay youth Smith had almost got knighted in 1763, who became mayor of the city in 1775 and again in 1790. Rush had bled and purged Powel to death, but he was seized with a maniacal fervor for his remedy, and in a letter informing his wife of

Powel's death, he said, "Never was the healing art so truly delightful to me!"

Philadelphians knew that the coming of cold weather somehow ended the yellow fever, and therefore the first of October was a hopeful sign, though the death rates were as high or higher than ever. The Smith family had been very lucky: only Nathaniel Blodget, Becky's brother-in-law, had died, and no one in the immediate family had even been sick. The beginning of October Becky, who had borne her first child only six weeks before, came down with it. She recovered, and before she was strong enough to escape to the country, her parents stopped in to visit her on Thursday, October 9. Returning home, said Smith, "My dear wife passing the gate of Christ Church burying ground, which then stood daily open, led me through it, to the graves of her two children; and calling the old gravedigger, marked a spot for herself. . . . By the side of her spot we found room and chose also mine, as it was not permitted during the sickness to open a grave once closed for the immediate burial of another."

Saturday, Mrs. Smith said she was "indisposed," but prevailed on her husband not to tell Becky, who was due to leave for Norristown the next day. Sunday, Mrs. Smith was really sick. "The poor Doctor alone remains with her," Rush wrote to his wife. Rush himself was having another bout of the fever and was too weak to come, but he sent assistants to bleed and purge in his name. Rush seems to have been especially close to the Smiths at this time: when many of his medical friends were becoming skeptical of his theories, the Smiths' loyalty seems to have overcome his puritanical revulsion to "the poor Doctor."

Mrs. Smith was sick a week. She was nursed by her

husband and by a fourteen-year-old black girl, though Primus may have been around the house somewhere. Then again he may have been out working in the streets: Philadelphia Negroes, led by the extraordinary Richard Allen, did work all out of proportion to their numbers, nursing the sick and carting and burying the fetid corpses, and got little but abuse for their trouble. On Friday Mrs. Smith was better, and Smith wrote to everyone to say that she was out of danger. On Sunday she died (for want of good nursing, said Rush). "She breathed her last," her husband wrote, "composed and patient, her countenance appearing to brighten, as her pangs and groans ceased, into the countenance of an angel. . . .

"Alas! how shall I live without her? I never had a joy which became a joy till she shared it. I never had a sorrow which she did not alleviate and participate—I never did an action which I considered as truly good till she confirmed my opinion— For my many failings and infirmities she had a friendly veil— Her conversation was enlightened, and that with her correspondence by letter, during my many absences, has been my joy for 35 years and more—"

The funeral was quick and quiet that same evening. Like all others who died in the plague, Mrs. Smith was put in a coffin and taken straight to the graveyard. No bells tolled. The only mourners were the coffinmaker, Smith, Primus, and Richard Allen. Without a light and perhaps even without a service she was lowered into her grave. The fever was clearly abating by then: the death rate had dropped to sixty, and would drop to twenty before the week was out. Every death is a death, nevertheless.

Smith wrote to all the children and to friends. He

wrote to Dr. Rush, two days later, a curiously garbled and touching letter, full of the random thoughts that would naturally concern a man at such a time: magnificent praise for his wife, acute descriptions of her sickness and death, maudlin ramblings about his own feelings, and not very honest observations about his investments. Next day his sister Isabella, who may have been forced to come into the city when Wolcott took over the house at the Falls, was down with the fever.

Isabella recovered (Smith didn't nurse her—he moved over to Becky's empty house), but on the 28th he was down with it himself. Taking Rush's purges as a preventive had weakened him, and he was soon only semi-coherent. "I am axtremly seiz'd with the fever— Last night I had a chill after going to for about three hours; but then fell asleep for a few hours if sleep it might where my imagination the living images of my dear wife and Mrs. Rogers my daughter Blodget sitting by me. . . ." But they went away, and he recovered too.

With the end of the fever in sight, Smith wrote an exhortation from the clergy to the citizens of Pennsylvania, urging them not to forget religion now that the plague was over; but it had to wait for publication until the clergy could get back to town and sign it. Over five thousand people had died in three months, or about ten percent of the population of the city, and there was no sense taking chances. The governments too, both state and federal, were slow to return. Washington was in Germantown October 28, but not until November 10 did he ride into the capital to have a look around. He did not take up residence again until December.

Between December and March, Smith preached a series of nine sermons in Christ Church. They were on "death, a resurrection from the dead, a future judgment, and an eternal world to come." They were lugubrious occasions, for religion—like butter on a burn—can salve if it is applied quickly, but can only fester if applied too late. Smith cried through the whole first sermon, and so did most of his listeners.

# 9 ❦ Old Age

Thomas Smith wrote of his brother in 1795, "He lives at his country-seat in a beautiful situation commanding a near view of the Schuylkill, five miles from the city. Our sister and he live there as if in an hermitage—I ride out occasionally to see him; but when a man has himself lost the enjoyment of life, another must relinquish it while in his presence—he has made an ample fortune—the children to whom it will devolve, would rejoice to see him enjoying his evening hours in the proper use of it; but as I frequently tell him, he never will."

Thomas Smith was benevolent but not profound, and he understood his brother hardly at all. Just as Julius Caesar was a young man all his life, projecting the perfection of himself and the world; just as Casanova was forever middle-aged, seeing his every escapade with detachment and restraint of judgment; so William Smith was born an old man. The devious self-denials with which the old excite our sympathies he mastered in youth, though he polished them further after his wife died; and he early commanded the crotchets of

manner and dress, the absorption in outworn triviali-
ties, the verbosity brooking no interruption, that flower
in most people only when their preoccupations with
sex and success have receded. Because he brought to old
age all of the devices with which the weak old contrive
to dominate the strong young, and because he even improved on them in the last ten years of his life, he became one of the most formidable old men of his time,
or of any time.

Not that he used his age to gain offices he had
been denied in youth: after his second expulsion from
the University of Pennsylvania, he never again held
high position in school or church or political life.
Rather, he used his age as a lever for getting his own
way, frequently saying, "If God continues me a little
longer," or "If health and opportunity permit." Yet
during this time he enjoyed remarkably good health:
he recovered from yellow fever in 1793, and from pleurisy in 1795. He was active and agile until his seventy-
fifth year, jumping up and running around like a youngster when he felt like it. He was able to make long and
arduous trips on horseback until very near the end, and
his stomach withstood the pickling he gave it until almost the day he died. In other words, though he mastered all the techniques of age, he was not really an old
man at all.

Smith's free tenancy of the provost's house ran out
in April, 1793, but as he did not then move out, the
trustees informed him that the rent would be £225 a
year. There is no evidence that he paid the slightest attention and, with the fever of that summer and fall, no
immediate effort was made to evict him. The next
spring, when he waited on the trustees indignantly to
tell them his annuity was in arrears, they paid him the

£100 but asked him for the house keys, assuring him that giving them up would not prejudice his claims. Assumedly, he was by then living mostly at the Falls, though retaining the house as a lever for his other claims. He was no longer demanding his teaching job, but only money.

The following spring, 1795, Smith and the trustees finally came to terms. A new committee was appointed to negotiate with him, and he at first told them he was entitled to (1) nine years' annuity, plus interest, 1779–88, (2) £130 he had advanced to pay for the orrery, (3) "the use and occupation of the house in which he now dwells, as being his property during life," and (4) nine years' provost's salary, or £2250, which would very nearly have bankrupted the university.

The committee went to Rittenhouse, who said that Smith had paid him no more than £107 (in another place he said £109/10), which Smith had gotten by giving the series of orrery lectures in 1771. What was worse, Rittenhouse had paid out £65 for cabinetry, leaving only £42, "which was all that I was ever paid for my labor." He did not, of course, mention the £300 that Assembly had paid him for the orrery, for Rittenhouse could be as disingenuous as Smith, and as self-righteous.

In April, Smith agreed to settle all his claims for £900 cash, plus the continuation of his annuity, which proved to be worth another £800 to him. A legal document was drawn up and signed. With that, he and Isabella—he called her Bell, and spelled it that way— moved what remained of their belongings out to the Falls, and Ewing moved back into the provost's house.

David Rittenhouse had been, during much of this time, director of the Mint. It was a political plum, a job requiring so little specialized knowledge that it was later awarded to Benjamin Rush, but it was at least a concrete job with concrete results, after the long, unproductive years as fumbling teacher and faltering scientist. Though he was now sixty-three, people still expected great things of him, and he had few more devoted admirers than Smith. However testy Rittenhouse might get, they were often thrown together. In 1786, when Smith was a commissioner for Maryland to confer on canals and Susquehanna navigation, Rittenhouse was a commissioner for Pennsylvania. Three years later, they were both charter members of the Society for Promoting the Improvement of Roads and Inland Navigation. In 1791, Governor Mifflin appointed them both agents of information under a new act to improve roads and waters. They made another surveying trip, and informed, and the next year the state finally decided to build a canal to connect the Schuylkill with the Susquehanna, and another to cut across just north of Philadelphia, from Fairmount to the Delaware.

Two companies were formed to dig these canals, and their memberships were almost identical—Robert Morris was president, and Smith, Rittenhouse, and a dozen others made up the boards. Smith merchandised some of the stock himself, in the same hustling manner he had used to get subscriptions for his two colleges. The members of the companies, the Philosophical Society, the businessmen of the city all realized that Philadelphia's future depended on the construction of these canals, and everyone took an interest. Washington, looking over Reading and Lancaster as possible seats of Congress if the yellow fever lingered in Philadelphia, made a detour to see how a lock on the Tulpehocken Creek was coming. Smith and an English engineer made a tour of inspection for the Schuylkill and Susquehanna Navigation Company the next year, and reported that four hundred men were at work, half of them on the Tulpehocken and the other half near Norristown; but progress was too slow and far too expensive.

A lottery was organized and Smith wrote a booklet in 1795 to promote the sale of stock, but still there just wasn't enought money. The companies were further hurt by the bankruptcy of their president, and the work slowed and stopped. Work was not resumed for twenty years, and then under a different company.

Smith was doubly a loser: he lost what he had invested, and he lost what his western lands would have appreciated, had the canal gone through. This canal had been only the first phase of a larger scheme, investigated by Smith and Rittenhouse in 1791 and approved by Assembly, to make a water connection all the way to Pittsburgh, with eighteen miles of portage. The route would have followed the Juniata, and would have passed right through Huntingdon.

In Huntingdon, Smith built a grist mill in 1792. He gave land for various churches and a school, and two cannon and a school bell in 1798. He tried to get a classicist sent out there to teach, but the young man decided to go to St. Croix instead. Smith liked Huntingdon, where the arrival of the proprietor was a great event, and whisky was always at hand. He was probably in a stupor much of the time he was there, and did some very erratic things. One day, he found a certain McCarthy, who wanted to build a chimney, loading stones from one of his fields into a cart. "Who gave thee orders to tak' these stanes?" said Smith.

"No one. I thought I was doing you a kindness."

"Dear mon, you have a queer way of showing me a

kindness; these are my stanes; throw them out, every one of them."

A few days later, Smith came upon another man, loading up a wagon with the same stones that McCarthy had put back. "Who gave thee orders to tak' these stanes?" said Smith.

"No one."

"Throw them out, every one of them; these are Henry McCarthy's stanes."

According to the story, told in a history of the McCarthy family, McCarthy came and got the stones, and Smith was "entirely satisfied."

Smith's difficulty in Huntingdon was his son Richard, who wanted to play the great man and surround himself with sycophants. Anybody who came by was invited to have a drink and stay to dinner, and it must have worried his father, who certainly hadn't brought him up that way. In fact, though we know many instances of Smith going to dinner here or there, there is no record of anybody ever having gone to dinner at the Smiths'.

Richard's extravagance went beyond the table. He decided he must build the handsomest house in Huntingdon, smack on the main street and opposite what had been, till then, the handsomest house in Huntingdon. He was "a gentleman of the old school," says a local historian, and probably most eighteenth-century gentlemen were as gaudy as he was. Fortunately, his father did not live to see the worst. Richard won an Assembly seat in 1803—after having been shellacked in 1795—and on his way to the capitol at Lancaster he was served for debt. He pleaded his privilege and could not then be taken, but as he could not stay at the capitol forever, his unfinished mansion was eventually sold by the court and brought about a tenth of what he had put into it. His library was taken too, though he himself does not seem to have gone to jail.

He was given a sinecure in the state government, but was pursued by a lawsuit in which he was charged with fraud as well as stupidity. The suit was pending for years, and when it finally came up, his nerves were not equal to it. Taunted by his adversary, he stood up, shaking, to defend himself. The judge ordered him to sit down, but in his confusion, rage, and fear, he did not hear, and spoke on until he was ordered down a third time. He did sit, and gradually his head slumped down on his chest, and then on his desk, and the court went on with the suit for several moments before it realized he was dead.

William Smith's last visit to Huntingdon, so far as we know, was in October, 1801, when he was seventy-four. The trip was hardly any easier than it had been forty years before—two hundred miles each way, nearly half of it on horseback, across rugged, broken country. But the town was an incorporated place now, with at least a hundred families paying quitrents on their lots, and innumerable acres beyond the borough adding their bit to his pocket every year. It has been claimed by some sentimentalists that Smith was "land poor" to the end of his days, and his numerous pleas of poverty are cited in support. But even if capital gain and income could be distinguished—and few investors would be so foolish as to try—he was still a rich man.

Smith was paid, at his own request, "the value of a teacup" for his series of sermons on the yellow fever—the church was strapped and what money it did have was spent on relief. Thereafter, he continued in demand as an occasional preacher: he gave the Masons their St. John's Day sermon, he presided over two general conventions of the church, he preached at the consecration of another bishop. In his *Works,* he says that he gave, "in substance," the same sermon that he gave for Claggett, which seems odd, as the two occasions were less than three years apart, and the two congregations must have been largely identical. But Smith, once he had given a performance that satisfied him, never hesitated to repeat it, as when he prescribed the same curriculum for Washington College that he had used for the College of Philadelphia.

After the failure of his episcopal ambitions and the rejection of most of his modifications to the prayer book, Smith was never again a power in the church. He retained what influence he had by his willingness to go on working with those who had opposed him, like William White and John Andrews. He was used to it—in the Philosophical Society, he had been forced to go on working with Franklin and Ewing after his quarrels with them, and in the College with Ewing and Andrews. Pennsylvania was still too small for men of like interests to avoid each other; and for Smith, quarrels—like friendships—were for life.

Smith wrote several pamphlets in his last years: "An Account of the Proceedings of the Illinois and Ouabache Land Companies," "An Account of the Conewago Canal, on the River Susquehanna," and "Remarks on a Second Publication by B. Henry Latrobe, Engineer." Latrobe's publication had been about Philadelphia drinking water, which was putrid and was suspected of having caused the second yellow fever epidemic, killing thirty-six hundred in 1798, and about a new scheme to bring Schuylkill water through pumping stations and mains to every part of the city. However, Latrobe wanted the water taken directly from the river, while Smith wanted it taken from the incompleted canal of the Delaware and Schuylkill Canal Company, of which he was still a member. In the pamphlet he showed himself as forceful and vindictive as ever; nevertheless it was Latrobe who built the waterworks.

The problem with being old was that, no matter how good health Smith enjoyed and how much he felt like doing, friends kept dying. Rittenhouse did it in 1796—he was five years younger than Smith, but had had an ulcer all his life, and hypochondria too—and two years later Jacob Duché did it. Of the five students who had surrounded and adored him forty years before, Duché, Hopkinson, Godfrey, and Evans were all dead, and West had been in London all his adult life. In 1799 his old and admired friend—indeed, perhaps in some ways his *best* friend—the American Cincinnatus died. In 1801, Elizabeth Graeme Fergusson died. "A woman of uncommon talents and virtues, admired, esteemed, and beloved," wrote Benjamin Rush. "I owe her many obligations." But Smith owed her even more.

Though many friends were dropping away, Smith's brother Thomas continued in good health and spirits. In 1795, at the age of fifty, he was appointed a justice of the Pennsylvania Supreme Court, where his rough manners were not all that out of place: one of the other justices smoked cigars from the bench. "Smith was defectively educated in the law, but by great industry he amassed a considerable knowledge of it," says Horace Binney, who—as a young lawyer—tried cases before him. "Mr. Rawle upon one occasion invited some of the bench and bar to dine with him at Harley, his summer residence near Falls of Schuylkill, and I was one of the number. It was a day in July, excessively hot, and the Ridge Road dusty to suffocation. I went with some of my young friends in a hackney coach, and we overtook Judge Smith on the road. He was on horseback, in enormous boots that came above his knees like a fisherman's, a cocked hat exposing his whole face to the fiery sun, and a full cloth dress which had been black probably when he set out, but when we saw him was almost a dirty drab. Some fifteen minutes after our arrival he came into the saloon where the company had assembled. His hat was then in his hand, but on his head was a mass of paste made by the powder and pomatum, a part of which had run down in white streams upon his face, as red in all the unplastered parts as a boiled lobster; and his immense boots and spurs, broad skirted coat, and the rest of the appearance I have described, made him the most extraordinary figure for a summer dinner that I have ever seen; but he did not appear to think that he was otherwise than he ought to be for the honor of his host, or for his own comfort."

William Smith, visiting Charles in Lancaster in 1800, fell sick and was a semi-invalid in January and February, but that didn't keep him from preaching the funeral sermon of his old neighbor, Governor Mifflin, who died in office. "The honor done to his name by this public funeral, and the vote of a monument by the legislature, to perpetuate his memory, will rescue his public virtue from public censure," said Smith. He was seventy-two years old now, and could say what he pleased.

Though Smith recovered his health, his sickness of that winter impressed upon him, as nothing else had done, the imminence of his own death. When he got back to the Falls, he began work to assure his terrestrial immortality: he arranged to have his portrait taken by Gilbert Stuart, he interested himself—through letters to friends—in fixing the details of incidents in his younger life, and he once again took up the publication of his sermons.

On the death of his wife, he had written to Rush, "For the rest of my days, few and they cannot be many —I would willingly devote them to discharge of some public engagements, by assorting and leaving to the world some sermons and other writings." But he had been too preoccupied with worldly business for the last seven years. The prospectus of 1789 had made the rounds of church conventions, and thirty-one delegates subscribed for copies. It was also circulated among friends and throughout the government, which gave him sixty-four more signatures, including George Washington's. It was not a large list, and many of these people had died in the last eleven years; still, he determined to go ahead with it.

Smith sold the Falls Tavern and his ferry rights, which had been leased out all these years. Perhaps the sale money was to pay for the marble mausoleum he now decided to build on his place: a mausoleum of the finest and most durable materials, surmounted by the statue of an angel carved by William—cousin of Benjamin—Rush. "Time shall be no more" was to be carved into the marble, for the benefit of those who could not read the longer inscriptions in Latin. This was the last of a long series of alterations and improvements to his property, and Smith watched the work closely. One day, making an inspection with Primus, he said, "I shall be buried there, but one like you cannot be."

"All right, Massah Smith, it won't matter," said Primus. "The devil will know where to find you wherever you are." In May, 1801, Primus died and was buried *out*side the mausoleum.

The same year, Isabella died and was buried *in*side. We know very little about her except that she had been in America a long time, had kept the house at the Falls while Smith was in Chestertown, and had been his only housekeeper since the death of his wife. She undoubtedly talked with the same Scottish burr that her two brothers never lost, and she seems to have conformed readily enough to Smith's pinch-penny domestic regimen. After her death Smith, whose eyesight was beginning to fail, was increasingly dependent on a certain German girl who, according to Dr. Rush, "not only robbed him, but often treated him with neglect and insult." Perhaps to escape her, he courted another woman, and even offered to settle money on her, but she refused him. By that time, his appearance was so slovenly that he must have made an odd suitor.

Meanwhile, he worked on preparing the sermons for the press. One of the pleasures they offered him was a last poke at Benjamin Franklin. As a postscript to the Franklin eulogy, he quoted a five stanza poem, which concluded,

> But to covet political fame
>   Was in him a degrading ambition;
> A spark which from Lucifer came,
>   Enkindled the blaze of sedition.
>
> Let candor then write on his urn—
>   "Here lies the renowned inventor,
> Whose flame to the skies ought to burn,
>   But inverted, descends to the center!"

Because of Smith's eyesight, an editor came out from town to help him, and he responded by giving the copyright to the editor, an act which cannot have cost him much. For a frontispiece to the first volume, he decided to use the Stuart portrait, and sent for David Edwin, a young engraver. "The doctor had been a schoolmaster," wrote Edwin, "and, although ignorant of the art of engraving, undertook to examine me on my capabilities. He was old, hasty, and very irritable. He began in a broad Scottish dialect, by asking me if I could draw. But when we came to the price of the plate, I thought the poor doctor would have gone distracted. He ran out and in the room, throwing at me angry and reproachful glances; and ended with the determination of paying me only half of my demand, which I accepted, considering the connection which I should form with Mr. Stuart by undertaking the work of more value to me than any sum the doctor could pay me for the plate."

Nonetheless, Edwin was miffed, and he retaliated by exaggerating every one of the old man's features: the nose is larger, the eyelids heavier, the hairs are fewer, the jowls more slack. Stuart painted Smith sober, but Edwin engraved him drunk. Smith had the last laugh: he never paid Edwin even the half price he talked him down to, and the bill was finally settled by his estate.

We do not know what William Smith died of. Benjamin Rush, to whom all diseases were one disease ("One of the great discoveries," wrote a pamphleteer, "which have contributed to the depopulation of the earth"), did not think Smith's particular symptoms worth remarking. To Rush, the one cause of all disease was "excessive excitability or spasm in the blood vessels," and therefore the one cure was bleeding. Smith, who grew weaker and weaker as he approached his final day, may simply have been bled to death.

He was sick in February, 1802, but recovered enough to preach at least once again, and to write his will. His estate he left in five equal portions: to his sons William Moore, Charles, and Richard, to Willy's children, and to three trustees who were to look after Becky's share. There were no specifications as to who was to get what—simply five shares "as near of equal value (quantity and quality considered) as can be estimated." He charged his children, "From regard to my memory, the education I have bestowed on them, my anxiety to provide for and assist them in gaining comfortable settlements in life, they will always preserve a mutual affection one to another." Fourteen gold mourning rings were to be made up and given to various people. The executors were to be his lawyer, his brother Thomas, his son Charles's father-in-law (a prominent judge), and Bishop White. When the executors learned of their honor, they thanked him but said they were too busy, so he appointed in their place his lawyer and his three lawyer sons.

Smith stayed at the Falls through the winter of 1802–3, attended often by Dr. Rush, who seems to have had less patients every year. Smith was confined to bed by February, but he went over the galleys of his sermons, and read over also the deeds to all his properties, as literature much more interesting to him than prayerbook or Bible, even though he knew all the measurements by heart. When his eyesight was too faint to read, he had William Moore Smith read the deeds to him, and corrected him if he made a single mistake. Even this entertainment was denied him when his son left for England in March, to be agent for British claimants in America.

In April, William Moore's wife Ann took him and all his papers down to her house in the city. The rector of Christ Church, coming to give him communion, asked him whether he had any self-reproaches, and he answered only that he might have been "a little too hasty in my temper." Though preparing for the end, he had rallied enough the beginning of May to be transacting business by letter with Charles, and to be going over his precious papers again. Still, he was uncomfortable, and sent notes to Rush, asking him—rather, commanding him—to come. Rush came, but Smith said, "By the Lord God, if you don't stay longer with me I will send for another doctor."

When his eyesight again failed him, Smith had his nurse spread his deeds out on his bedspread so that he could gaze at their shapes, if not their substance, through the gathering haze. The last day, he was entirely blind, but still he wanted his papers. The nurse, perhaps because she could not find them or perhaps from pure contempt, put a couple of old medical papers into his trembling hands, and he fondled them for an hour before he died. It was May 14, 1803, and he was seventy-six. As soon as he heard, Bishop White came and took away all the ecclesiastical papers, which Smith had kept in a separate box. Some of them have survived.

The first two volumes of Smith's sermons were published shortly after his death. In a preface, the editor said he felt obliged to go on with the remaining volumes (there were to be many, for Smith had plans to publish everything he had ever written) without waiting to see how the first two sold. However, no more were ever published. Had Smith lived, he would have pushed sales, and the series would have continued; but when he was dead, no one was interested in reading his sermons, because they read the author too well.

Smith was buried in his mausoleum. A number of Episocopalian preachers attended, following the hearse out Ridge Avenue in a long string of dusty carriages, but none of his children could make it. Richard was in Huntingdon, Charles in Lancaster, William Moore in England, Becky God knows where. Bishop White read the service, but there was no memorable sermon, no eulogy delivered to the Philosophical Society. Horace Wemyss Smith was perplexed and hurt that his great-grandfather's funeral should have been so spare, and wrote to a neighbor who had recently published a history of the Falls of Schuylkill, which mentioned every millwright, shad fisherman, and day laborer who had ever passed through town, but never mentioned William Smith. Yes, the historian answered, he remembered Dr. Smith: as a boy he had seen him often, but he didn't remember anything about the funeral. Sorry.

What had William Smith done to that boy? What did he do to nearly everyone he met? His sermons didn't sell, after his death, and his many virtues and talents were soon forgotten by all who had known him because Smith lived his life not for others, nor even for what others might think of him, but absolutely for *himself;* and once such a life is over, most people would just as soon forget it.

Dr. Rush, for all his quackery, was observant of human nature, and was on the whole a good friend of Smith's. In his commonplace book, he wrote on the day Smith died, "This man's life and character would fill a volume. He was a native of Scotland, and arrived in Philadelphia above 50 years ago, and for many years made a distinguished figure in the politics of Pennsylvania. He possessed genius, taste, and learning. As a teacher he was perspicuous and agreeable, and as a preacher solemn, eloquent, and expressive in a high degree. Unhappily his conduct in all his relations and situations was opposed to his talents and profession. . . . He appears to have been a nondescript in the history of man."

By *nondescript*, Rush meant not a man without identity, but rather a man without precedent. But is it true? Surely all of us have dreamed to live as Smith did: he knew what he wanted, and he managed to get most of it. His life had reverses, and it was in some ways shallow and even ludicrous, but it was long and was filled with pleasures that to lesser minds seem contradictory —the stimulations of science and teaching and good company, the exaltations of literature and liquor, the assurances of family and money and religion. Smith did almost everything that is worth doing in the world: enjoyed a woman and helped her become a women he could enjoy more, raised himself from the most squalid beginnings to real eminence, cut a figure in high places without tailoring himself to that figure—often without even shaving or changing his clothes. He met everyone worth meeting in his time and place, and he knew the city, the country, the wilderness, land and water, the heavens, all plants and animals. What more does anyone get from three score and ten, even with six years' interest?

It is sad how little of William Smith survives today. The buildings with which he was most intimately associated are all gone: Whitefield's Tabernacle of the College of Philadelphia was razed in the nineteenth century. Washington College burned, and the replacement buildings are in a different and less grandiose manner. His house at the Falls yielded to an apartment yet to be built, and the provost's house to a concrete honeycomb. His two churches, Trinity in northeast Philadelphia and Emanuel in Chestertown, are still standing, but Victorianized beyond recognition. There is Christ Church, of course, and Independence Hall itself, and hundreds of other buildings in Philadelphia and Chestertown that he must have known, but none with which he was closely connected. His town of Huntingdon, though no longer a proprietorship, has survived and grown, and his street plan is still adhered to, but none of the buildings date from his time.

None of his writing is read, or is likely to be read soon. The eloquence that Smith commanded he employed topically, and there are too many good books in the language to read another for its eloquence alone. Likewise his plan of education, first put forth in *A College of Mirania,* may occasionally be dipped into by a pedant trying to write *Doctor* cheaply before his name, but no rigid curriculum can be said to have shaped American education today.

As a teacher, few can have been better than Smith, but whatever it is that a teacher creates, it does not last many years beyond his own time. The same can be said of a preacher, in spades.

Two biographies have been written of Smith: one by his great-grandson, and one by a graduate student in the pay of his descendants. It is pleasing to think of Smith's family, so long after his death, still so devoted to him, and something of his cantankerous spirit may survive in them yet. But for those who would really like to learn about the man, it is more profitable to pick up a volume of eighteenth century letters or memoirs—for example, the Franklin papers dealing with Smith would make a book in themselves, if collected, and every page would be rich with incident and outrage. Or pick almost any other—pick Washington, Jefferson, Adams—and there Smith is, as vivid as if he still lived: belting the militia captain, guarding the rare map, aspiring to the sleeves.


Manayunk
1970–71

# Chronology

1727  William Smith born
1743  enters University of Aberdeen
1747  begins teaching school
1751  emigrates to Long Island
1753  writes *A College of Mirania*
1755  becomes first provost of College
      of Philadelphia
1757  buys first parcel of land at the Falls
      of Schuylkill
1758  jailed for printing libel of Assembly.
      Marries Rebecca Moore.
1762–64  in England soliciting endowment for College
1766  becomes rector of Trinity Church
1767  lays out town of Huntingdon
1769  observes transit of Venus
1774  member of Committee of Correspondence
1776  preaches to Congress on death of
      General Montgomery
1777–78  British occupation of Philadelphia
1780  moves to Chestertown
1782  founds Washington College
1783  elected Bishop of Maryland
1785  revises prayer book
1789  returns to Philadelphia
1791  eulogy on Franklin
1792  not hired by University of Pennsylvania
1793  yellow fever
1795  writes book on canal navigation
1800  preaches at funeral of General Mifflin
1803  William Smith dies

# Family Tree

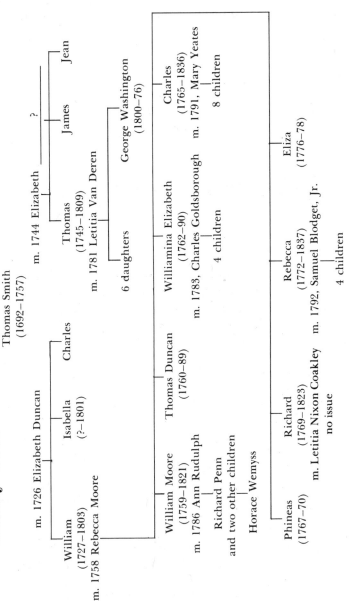

# Bibliography

Africa, J. Simpson. *History of Huntingdon and Blair Counties*. Philadelphia: L. H. Everts, 1883.

*American Magazine and Monthly Chronicle*. Philadelphia: William Bradford, 1757–58.

American Philosophical Society. *Transactions*. vol. 1. Philadelphia: American Philosophical Society, 1769.

Barton, William. *Memoirs of David Rittenhouse*. Philadelphia: Parker, 1813.

Bridenbaugh, Carl. *Mitre and Sceptre*. New York: Oxford University Press, 1962.

Bridenbaugh, Carl and Jessica. *Rebels and Gentlemen*. New York: Reynal and Hitchcock, 1942.

Chamberlain, Joshua Lawrence. *Universities and Their Sons: University of Pennsylvania*. 2 vols. Boston: Herndon Co., 1902.

Cheyney, Edward Potts. "Archives General—Dr. William Smith's Claim, 1792–95." Manuscript in the archives of the University of Pennsylvania.

——— *History of the University of Pennsylvania*. Philadelphia: University of Pennsylvania Press, 1940.

Evans, Nathaniel. *Poems On Several Occasions*. Philadelphia: John Dunlop, 1772.

Ford, Edward. *David Rittenhouse, Astronomer-Patriot.* Philadelphia: University of Pennsylvania Press, 1946.

Fox, Bertha Sprague. "Provost William Smith and his Land Investments in Pennsylvania." *Pennsylvania History 8* (1941): 189–209.

Franklin, Benjamin. *Papers.* 14 vols. to date, and more forthcoming. New Haven: Yale University Press, 1959– .

————— *Writings.* 10 vols. New York: Macmillan, 1905–07.

Galt, John. *The Life of Benjamin West.* Reprint. Gainesville: Scholars' Facsimiles and Reprints, 1960.

Gegenheimer, Albert Frank. *Provost William Smith and His Group."* Manuscript in the University of Pennsylvania library.

————— *William Smith: Educator and Churchman.* Philadelphia: University of Pennsylvania Press, 1943.

Godfrey, Thomas. *Juvenile Poems On Various Subjects.* Philadelphia: Henry Miller, 1765.

Hagner, Charles V. *Early History of the Falls of Schuylkill.* Philadelphia: Claxton, 1869.

Hindle, Brooke. *David Rittenhouse.* Princeton: Princeton University Press, 1964.

Konkle, B. A. *Life and Times of Thomas Smith.* Philadelphia: Campion, 1904.

*Maryland Historical Magazine.* Baltimore: Maryland Historical Society, 1906– .

Mills, Charles K. *Falls of Schuylkill.* Philadelphia: University of Pennsylvania Press, 1920 (?).

Nolan, J. Bennett. *The Only Franklin in Franklin's College.* Philadelphia: Philadelphia Graphic Arts Forum, 1939.

————— *The Schuylkill.* New Brunswick: Rutgers University Press, 1951.

*Pennsylvania Magazine of History and Biography.* Philadelphia: Historical Society of Pennsylvania, 1877– .

Perry, William Stephens. *Historical Collections Relating to* the American Colonial Church. 4 vols. Reprint. New York: AMS Press, 1969.

———— History of the American Episcopal Church. Boston: J. R. Osgood, 1885.

Powell, John H. *Bring Out Your Dead*. Philadelphia: University of Pennsylvania Press, 1949.

Reath, Henry T. *Ebb Tide at Philadelphia*. Manuscript in the Historical Society of Pennsylvania.

Rightmyer, Nelson Waite. *Maryland's Established Church*. Baltimore: Church Historical Society for the Diocese of Maryland, 1956.

Rush, Benjamin. *Autobiography*. ed. Corner. Princeton: Princeton University Press, 1948.

———— *Letters*. ed. Butterfield. 2 vols. Princeton: Princeton University Press, 1951.

Scharf, J. Thomas. *History of Maryland*. Reprint. Detroit: Gale, 1967.

Scharf, J. Thomas and Westcott, Thomson. *History of Philadelphia*. 3 vols. Philadelphia: L. H. Everts, 1884.

Stillé, C. J. *Memoir of the Rev. William Smith*. Philadelphia: Moore, 1869.

Smith, Horace Wemyss. *Life and Correspondence of Rev. William Smith, D.D.* Philadelphia: Claxton, 1880.

Smith, William. *Works*. 2 vols. Philadelphia: Maxwell and Fry, 1803.

———— *Account of the College, Academy, and Charitable School of Philadelphia*. Reprint. Philadelphia: University of Pennsylvania Library, 1951.

———— *An Account of Washington College*. Philadelphia: Crukshank, 1784.

———— *The Collection Books of Provost Smith*. ed. Brinton and Westlake. Facsimile. Philadelphia: University of Pennsylvania Press, 1964.

———— *An Examination of the Connecticut Claim to Lands in Pennsylvania*. Philadelphia: Crukshank, 1774.

———— *An Historical Account of the Expedition Against*

*the Ohio Indians, in the Year 1764.* Philadelphia: William Bradford, 1765.

———— *An Historical Account of the Rise, Progress, and Present State of the Canal Navigation in Pennsylvania.* Philadelphia: Zachariah Poulson, 1795.

———— *Plain Truth.* Philadelphia and London: J. Almon, 1776.

Van Doren, Carl. *Benjamin Franklin.* New York: Viking, 1938.

Washington, George. *Writings.* 39 vols. Washington: Government Printing Office, 1931–40.

# ✿ Index

# 210 🦂 *Index*

In writing a serialized *History of Philadelphia,* five years ago, Thomas Firth Jones recognized that William Smith and Stephen Girard were both funny enough and serious enough to deserve readable biographies. He hopes to start on Girard soon, but right now he is working on an adventure novel with a Mexican setting.

Jones was born in Philadelphia in 1934, and has lived there most of his life. He is a graduate of Washington College and a union carpenter. He enjoys gardening, travel, motorcycle racing, and white water canoeing. His published writing includes a novel, *Stairway to the Sea,* and a motorcycling manual, *Enduro.*

Praise for *How Westminster Works*

'Lacerating . . . a savage indictment of the status quo. In a series of deeply informed and carefully worked out examples, Dunt takes us through the Westminster labyrinth to reveal an omnishambles'                                    *Guardian*

'Excellent . . . Dunt's analysis is refreshingly focused on reality, rather than academic abstraction. When he advocates change, it is because his book has shown how an existing set of incentives is ensuring failure. Read it and you will see just how deep our problems run'                              *New Statesman*

'Dunt has spent years watching Westminster and his book offers a comprehensive analysis of the problems with these institutions . . . far scarier than any conspiracy theory'
*The Times*

'An acute observer of what's gone wrong with our politics and why'                                              Alastair Campbell

'In clear, reasonable tones Dunt lays out why we should all be bloody furious at how badly British politics serves us . . . This is both an articulate wail of lament and a rousing call to arms'                                              Armando Iannucci

'A blistering account of the irrationality and sheer absurdity of Britain's dysfunctional political system . . . If you want to understand why this country is in such an almighty mess – and what we might do to fix it – read this book'
Caroline Lucas

'With typical incision, wit and flair, Dunt masterfully deconstructs and skewers our corrosive political culture. An indispensable analysis of how we got into this mess'

The Secret Barrister

'A devastating diagnosis of how Britain's political engine has broken down. Everyone in Westminster should read it'

Oliver Bullough, author of *Butler to the World*

'Thrilling, searing and scathing, but ultimately hopeful that our political system can be rescued from the quagmire'

Adam Rutherford, author of
*How to Argue with a Racist*

'A brilliant, surgical book . . . An angry and clear exposition of a system that doesn't make sense'

Isabel Hardman, author of
*Why We Get the Wrong Politicians*

'Hugely entertaining and informative . . . A must-read for anyone who cares about British politics, where we are at and where we should be going'

Otto English, author of *Fake History*

'The inner workings of Westminster are undeniably important, but making them interesting takes talent – commentators like Ian Dunt are rare and valuable things'

Tom Chivers, author of *How to Read Numbers*